MANAGEMENT INTELLIGENCE

MANAGEMENT INTELLIGENCE

Sense and nonsense for the successful manager

Adrian Furnham

palgrave
macmillan

First published 2008 by
PALGRAVE MACMILLAN
Houndmills, Basingstoke, Hampshire RG21 6XS and
175 Fifth Avenue, New York, N.Y. 10010
Companies and representatives throughout the world

PALGRAVE MACMILLAN is the global academic imprint of the Palgrave Macmillan division of St. Martin's Press, LLC and of Palgrave Macmillan Ltd. Macmillan® is a registered trademark in the United States, United Kingdom and other countries. Palgrave is a registered trademark in the European Union and other countries.

ISBN-13: 978–0–230–21664–8
ISBN-10: 0–230–21664–1

This book is printed on paper suitable for recycling and made from fully managed and sustained forest sources. Logging, pulping and manufacturing processes are expected to conform to the environmental regulations of the country of origin.

A catalogue record for this book is available from the British Library.

A catalog record for this book is available from the Library of Congress.

10   9   8   7   6   5   4   3   2   1
17   16   15   14   13   12   11   10   09   08

Printed and bound in China

To my primary support team
Alison and Benedict
of whom I am so proud

Contents

List of Tables

Preface

This book of short essays examines many beliefs and practices of good and bad managers. It hopes to review some latest thinking, dispel myths and provide insights.

There were three reasons for the book's title. The first arose from the frenzied quest to find new intelligences sparked off by the multiple intelligence gurus. Although the idea can be traced back to the 1920s, various educationists told people exactly what they wanted to hear despite there being little or no evidence for these assertions. First, that intelligence as measured in the academic, IQ sense, was limited. Second, that there were many types of intelligence and that it was likely that everyone was (at least) good at something. This was the "everyone-must-have-a-prize" school of education.

It was the "discovery" of emotional intelligence that really triggered the crazed quest to find other "intelligences." Academic bestseller writers and business gurus all found that old and even long-dismissed ideas could be happily repackaged and sold off or converted to "intelligence." So charm became social skills which in turn became emotional intelligence.

Intelligence became a synonym for skill or competency. So why not "management intelligence"? That is ability, skill, disposition (or whatever) to be good at managing others. The second reason for the title is the use of the word "intelligence" in the military or business sense. Thus one has intelligence about new, emerging markets or about competitor (or enemy) intentions. *The Economist* magazine has its Intelligence Unit which provides wonderfully detailed and informative reports on a wide range of topics. Known for their factual accuracy, depth and analysis they are a model of business intelligence research.

To be in the intelligence corps of any military is usually a sign of being particularly talented -- possibly linguistically or cryptographically. While jokes are made about the oxymoronic nature of the concept of "military intelligence" there are numerous examples of battles, indeed whole wars, being won primarily because of the superior knowledge of one side about the intentions and capabilities of the other.

It would be both wrong and pretentious to believe that this book is packed full of management intelligence. However, many essays are either research-based or research-informed and topics are chosen to stimulate thought and analysis. I hope at least to dispel various myths about management.

The third reason for the title is that it is ironic. As noted in the introduction the skeptic may point out that the discovery of all these new intelligences is little more than a hearty mixture of fashion and marketing. So why not call finding a partner through speed-dating or lonely-heart-club correspondence "sexual intelligence"? Or why not call all the nasty, backstabbing and maneuvering at work for senior positions "promotional intelligence"?

So the third reason for the title is to convey irony, even sarcasm. This book does take a sideways glance at the management. It is difficult not to be amazed and amused by the daft, delusional or dimwitted ideas of some managers or of some of those who write about the topic. At worst they are desperately naïve about people and/or the benefits of certain approaches. They are also frequently very misleading. They dumb down rather than lift up. This is what makes the word "intelligence" so ironic.

Some of these essays have been described as naughty. Some have appeared in different guises in newspaper columns and have "excited debate." That is they have attracted everything from thanks to hate mail. Puncturing pomposity causes strong reactions.

But I hope the tone is not entirely ironic or negative. The aim is to use humor to question ideas, motives or approaches.

The essays have been written in many places and conceived in many more. Airport lounges, holiday beaches and long train journeys seem good places to do a spot of scribbling while (relatively) undisturbed. Unashamedly all written by hand, they are carefully processed before appearing, having to pass through the "critical judge" experience of my talented wife who might demand anything from a full rewrite to an immediate discard. It is the point where impetuous impulsivity meets the wall of obsessional carefulness. And the book is better for it.

The essays are like tablets: to be taken a few at a time. They are designed to cure hangovers, reduce blood pressure and lighten the mood. They are also meant to be prophylactics against managerial madness. Take two, then call me/email me in the morning.

ADRIAN FURNHAM
a.furnham@ucl.ac.uk

Introduction – intelligence at work

Social intelligence (SI)

Psychologists have long been interested in the "social intelligences." These are nearly always put in inverted commas because, strictly speaking, they are not intelligences but conceived of as social skills, even dispositions, that have both multiple causes and multiple consequences.

There are many explanations for interest in the "social intelligences." One is that cognitive ability (that is, academic intelligence) rarely explains more than a third to a half of the variance in any outcome measure, such as academic achievement, job performance or health. The question is, do the social intelligences predict management effectiveness better than do IQ test results? A second explanation is that intelligence has been recognized, but it has been demonstrated that it is difficult to improve or teach cognitive ability. Third, for over twenty years new advocates of "multiple intelligence" have been enormously successful in persuading people both of their existence and importance, despite the quality of their empirical evidence.

Mackintosh (1998) sees SI as social competence and success in social interactions. He argues that it is adaptive and can be seen in other animal species. It allows individuals to understand others' hopes, fears, beliefs and wishes.

He believes that is not too difficult to define social intelligence (mainly in terms of social skills) or indeed to devise tests to measure it. But he doubts two things: first, whether these many social and interpersonal skills actually load on a single dimension, and second whether they are uncorrelated with, and therefore related to, standard IQ measures of cognitive ability.

Various researchers have believed SI to be multifunctional, relating to such issues as social sensitivity, social insight and social communication. In other words it is much more of a social or personality variable than a cognitive variable, which is more about information processing and accumulation. Hence "trait emotional intelligence." Over the past decade or so there has been an explosion in the number of "multiple intelligences"

Table I.1 The many identified multiple intelligences

	Multiple intelligence	Author	Year
1.	Analytical	Sternberg	1997
2.	Bodily-kinesthetic	Gardner	1999
3.	Creative	Sternberg	1997
4.	Emotional	Salovey and Mayer	1990
5.	Interpersonal	Gardner	1999
6.	Intrapersonal	Gardner	1999
7.	Mathematical	Gardner	1999
8.	Musical	Gardner	1999
9.	Naturalistic	Gardner	1999
10.	Practical	Sternberg	1997
11.	Sexual	Conrad and Milburn	2001
12.	Spatial	Gardner	1999
13.	Spiritual	Emmons	2000
14.	Verbal	Gardner	1999

discovered. Hardly a year goes by before yet another is discovered. Table I.1 shows fourteen "different intelligences."

Among academic researchers social intelligences are not usually considered part of cognitive ability, and "intelligences" is always put in inverted commas. There are two reasons for this: first, there is very little good, empirical evidence supporting the idea that these are separate factors, distinguishable from each other; second, they seem unrelated to traditional measures of intelligence. More interesting, a variety of studies have shown that laypeople believe that a number of the multiple intelligences (for example musical, bodily-kinesthetic, emotional) are *not* linked to traditional ideas of intelligence.

The two figures most powerfully involved with the multiple intelligence world are Sternberg (1997) and Gardner (1983, 1999). Gardner (1983) defined intelligence as "the ability to solve problems or to create products that are valued within one or more cultural settings" (p. 11) and specified seven intelligences. He argued that *linguistic-verbal* and *logical-mathematical intelligences* are those typically valued in educational settings. Linguistic intelligence involves sensitivity to the spoken and written language and the ability to learn languages. Logical-mathematical intelligence involves the capacity to analyze problems logically, solve mathematical problems and investigate issues scientifically. These two types of intelligence dominate intelligence tests. Three other multiple intelligences are arts-based: *musical intelligence* which refers to skill in the performance, composition and appreciation of musical patterns; *bodily kinesthetic intelligence* which is based on the use of the whole or parts of the body to solve problems or to fashion products; and *spatial intelligence* which is the ability to recognize and manipulate patterns in space. There are also two personal intelligences: *interpersonal intelligence* which is the capacity to understand the intentions, motivations and desires of other people and to work effectively with them; and *intrapersonal intelligence* which is the capacity to understand oneself and to use this information effectively in regulating one's life.

However, in his later book Gardner (1999) defines intelligence as a "biopsychological potential to process information that can be activated in a cultural setting to solve problems or create products that are of value in a culture" (pp. 33–4). He introduces three possible new intelligences, although he notes: "The strength of the evidence for these varies, and whether or not to declare a certain human capacity another type of intelligence is certainly a judgement call" (p. 47). However he adds only one new intelligence, namely *naturalistic intelligence*, which is "expertise in the recognition and classification of the numerous species – the flora and fauna – of [the subject's] environment" (p. 43). It is the capacity for taxonomization: for recognizing members of a group, for distinguishing among members of a species and for charting out the relations, formally or informally, among several species. The other two are spiritual and existential intelligences. *Spiritual intelligence* is the ability to master a set of diffuse and abstract concepts about being, but also mastering the craft of altering one's consciousness in attaining a certain state of being. This has recently become an issue of considerable debate (Emmons 2000). *Existential intelligence* is yet more difficult to define:

> [T]he capacity to locate oneself with respect to the furthest reaches of the cosmos – the infinite and infinitesimal – and the related capacity to locate oneself with respect to such existential features of the human condition as the significance of life, the meaning of death, the ultimate fate of the physical and the psychological worlds and such profound experiences as love of another person or total immersion in a work of art. (Gardner 1999, p. 61)

It should be pointed out however that despite its popularity in educational circles, Gardner's theory has been consistently attacked and criticized by those working empirically in the area who believe in *g* – as general intelligence.

Until comparatively recently there had been no real attempt to provide empirical evidence for multiple intelligence theory. However, Visser *et al.*

tested 200 participants, giving them 8 tests of the Gardner intelligences. They concluded: "Results support previous findings that highly diverse tests of purely cognitive abilities share strong loadings on a factor of general intelligence and that abilities involving sensory, motor or personality influences are less strongly g-loaded" (p. 487). Later they wrote:

> The substantial *g*-loadings of all purely cognitive tests in the current study contradict Gardner's assertion that there are at least eight independent intelligence domains. Although Gardner has acknowledged the existence of *g* and has conceded that the eight intelligences might not be entirely independent, his contention that positive correlations between various cognitive tasks are largely due to verbal demands was clearly not supported in this study, in which those verbal demands were minimised. Instead, measures of Linguistic, Spatial, Logical-Mathematical, Naturalistic, and Interpersonal intelligences showed a positive manifold of correlations, substantial loadings on a *g* factor, and substantial correlations with an outside measure of general intelligence. The common element that saturated the highly *g* loaded tests most strongly was their demand on reasoning abilities, not their specifically verbal content.
>
> The finding that several of the partly non-cognitive tests in this study were very weakly *g*-loaded is unsurprising, and suggests that Gardner is likely correct in claiming that Bodily-Kinesthetic ability is quite different from the various cognitive abilities. Given the important contribution of non-cognitive as well as cognitive abilities to performance in the Bodily-Kinesthetic, Musical and Intrapersonal domains, "talents" might be a more appropriate label than "intelligences."
>
> Finally, some of the ability domains proposed by Gardner were not supported by the present data, as the within-domain correlations were either very weak (Bodily-Kinesthetic, Intrapersonal) or attributable entirely to *g* (Naturalistic). The coherence of some of the other ability domains (e.g. Linguistic, Spatial), as shown by significant residual correlations after the extraction of *g*, is consistent with Multiple Intelligences theory. However, this result is explained equally well by the much older hierarchical models of intelligence, which postulate several group factors in addition to an important *g* factor. (p. 501)

Sternberg (1997) has developed a multidimensional model, also known as the "triarchic" theory of "successful" intelligence. This posits that human intelligence comprises three aspects, namely, componential, experiential and contextual. The *componential* aspect refers to a person's ability to learn new things, to think analytically and to solve problems. This aspect of intelligence is manifested through better performance on standard intelligence tests, which require general knowledge and ability in areas such as arithmetic and vocabulary. The *experiential* aspect refers to a person's ability to combine different experiences in unique and creative ways. It concerns original thinking and creativity in both the arts and the sciences. Finally, the *contextual* aspect refers to a person's ability to deal with practical aspects of the environment and to adapt to new and changing contexts. This aspect of intelligence resembles what lay people sometimes refer to as "street smarts." Sternberg (1997) popularized these concepts and refers to them as analytic, creative and practical intelligence.

However, practical intelligence theory has also attracted very serious criticism. Gottfredson (2003), in an extremely exhaustive review of all the work in the area, disputes Sternberg's central claim that there exists a general factor of practical intelligence (made up of the three intelligences) that is distinct from academic intelligence as usually conceived. She concludes:

> It is true that *g* provides only a partial explanation of "intelligent behaviour," and that its role in everyday affairs is yet poorly understood. But there is a solid, century-long evidentiary base upon which researchers are busily building. Simply positing a new and independent intelligence to explain much of what remains unexplained (and much of what has *already* been explained), while simultaneously ignoring the ever-growing evidentiary base, does not promise to advance knowledge. The concept of tacit knowledge does, I suspect, point to a form of experience and knowledge that lends itself to the development of what might be called wisdom – a gradual understanding of the probabilities and possibilities in human behavior (and in individual persons) that we generally develop only by experiencing or observing them first-hand over the course of our lives. This is not a new form of intelligence, however, but perhaps only the motivated and sensitive application of whatever level of *g* we individually possess. Sternberg *et al.* could better advance scientific knowledge on this issue by probing more deeply and analytically into the role of tacit knowledge in our lives rather than continuing to spin gauzy illusions of a wholly new intelligence that defies the laws of evidence. (p. 392)

The idea of multiple intelligences seems to have been warmly embraced in the business world. Riggio *et al.* (2002) note that the multiple intelligence idea is intuitively appealing because it is self-evident that people require various areas of competence, other than only academic intelligence, to succeed at business leadership. Most organizations have a competency framework used in selection, assessment and appraisal, and all have specific multiple (often between six and eight) competencies that are desirable/required to do the job. They nearly always involve cognitive ability and other skills.

The reason for human resource specialists and others favouring the idea of multiple and social intelligences is due partly to caution using traditional tests. With litigation issues concerning test bias and a general dislike of cognitive ability tests, despite their proven validity, many have turned to multiple intelligence tests, such as they exist.

The concept of multiple intelligences, particularly emotional intelligence, has become extremely popular. Academic research has begun to "catch up" with this wave of interest by trying to define and measure it. More importantly for the topic of this book, researchers have begun to test the central claim that it adds incremental validity over conventional intelligence tests in predicting success at work, however measured.

Business or managerial intelligence

In a study of impatriate managers, Harvey *et al.* (2002) listed eight "managerial intelligences." They took as their starting-point Sternberg's (1985) triarchic theory of intelligence, but split the three intelligences further. Thus *analytic* intelligence is split into cognitive and emotional intelligence; *practical* intelligence into political, sociocultural, organizational and network intelligence; and *creative* intelligence into innovative and intuitive intelligence. Clearly this classification is controversial: for many researchers in the field, emotional intelligence is not part of general or cognitive intelligence.

These authors argue that cognitive IQ is the "g" factor of general intelligence that measures problem-solving abilities. They categorize emotional intelligence within the analytic category because "emotional development and maturity are viewed as necessary to allow managers to effectively utilize their cognitive abilities. The importance of emotional intelligence increases with the level of authority in an organization."

The four practical intelligences are, inevitably, more controversial. *Political IQ* is defined as

> the ability to gain resources through exercising political power in situations where ambiguity and accountability levels allow for a shaping (i.e. spin) of attitudes and images among those being influenced . . . A high political IQ refers to having a sense about the social infrastructure and the individuals that occupy

key positions that can be instrumental in exercising influence to change resource allocation or direction of the decision making. (p. 506)

Sociocultural IQ is really cultural knowledge and ability to translate or integrate specific cues about culture. *Organizational intelligence* is knowledge of how things are done via policies, procedures, planning processes and audits. It is, in effect, an understanding of the official formal rules of the organization and the ability to get things done in a specific organizational context. *Network intelligence* is essentially about inter-organizational management, while organizational IQ is about intra-organizational IQ. *Management IQ* is based on the size, structure and centrality of an individual's personal relationships across organizations.

According to Harvey *et al.* (2002), the two creative intelligences are innovative and intuitive intelligences. *Innovative intelligence* is defined quite specifically as

the ability to think in abstract terms, to develop business ideas and concepts that have not been conceptualized by others, constitutes business innovation. The embodiment of ideas/concepts into new processes, products, services and technologies is a valuable outcome of innovation. (p. 511)

Intuitive intelligence seems harder to define, and the authors talk about its "subconscious origin," "tacit nature," "street smarts," "sixth sense" and "gut knowledge."

The authors provide a profile that allows somebody to score individuals on their eight intelligences. They do *not*, however, provide any data for their theory that supports the threefold classification. More importantly, they make little attempt to distinguish between abilities and traits or to consider whether it is possible to train or develop these intelligences. Interestingly, nearly all the measures they propose for each of the IQs, save cognitive intelligence, are measured by self-report tests of preference, rather than power-based ability tests. Nevertheless, people recognize these different abilities/skills and traits.

One of the advantages of Harvey *et al.*'s (2002) description of managerial intelligences is that they employ psychological and psychometric concepts in the language of business.

The concept of business IQ, at least as outlined by Harvey *et al.* (2002), has yet to attract much attention. Certainly there remains little evidence of the separate "unique" existence of these intelligences or indeed that they predict anything.

Table I.2　Harvey's *et al.*'s questionnaire

	Type of IQ	Description
1.	Cognitive	The traditional measure of intellectual ability. This IQ measures the ability to reason, learn and think analytically.
2.	Emotional	The ability to use one's own affective state to tap the affective state of others to accomplish objectives. The ability to display an appropriate emotional state and to respond to others' emotions in an effective manner.
3.	Political	The ability to use the formal and informal power in the company to accomplish objectives. The ability to know how to prudently, judiciously and artfully use power in the organization.
4.	Social/Cultural	The extent to which one is adequately socialized in a society, an organization, or a subculture. Recognition and understanding of roles, norms, routines and taboos, in various settings.
5.	Organizational	Having a detailed and accurate understanding of how the organization operates both functionally and the time that is needed to accomplish certain tasks in the company. The detailed knowledge of how to "get things done" in the company.
6.	Network	The ability to get things done with multiple organizational units. Accomplishing the goals of the company effectively by recognizing, understanding and managing inter-organizational relations.
7.	Creative	The ability to diverge/innovate in thinking and create fresh novel ideas and solutions to problems. The ability to address problems/issues with insight and resourcefulness and to find unique solutions.
8.	Intuitive	The ability to have quick insights into how to solve problems or to address situations without past experience of the problem, and without formally processing information (for example street smart).

However, Furnham (2005) asked working adults to rate themselves, their boss, and their boss's boss on these eight intelligences. He found males rated their overall IQ as well as their cognitive, creative and political intelligence as significantly higher than females. Females rated their boss's overall, emotional and organizational IQ significantly higher than did male participants. Participants believed they had higher emotional intelligence than their boss, but lower political, organizational and network intelligence. Regressions indicated that only one of the eight estimated business intelligences (cognitive intelligence) was related to overall (total, general) estimated intelligence in self, boss or boss's boss.

Once again, although these concepts are immensely appealing to consultants and managers themselves, it is essentially misleading to label them "intelligences." It would be more sensible to call these competencies. The question, rarely asked, but nevertheless very important, is, what is the origin of such "intelligences"/competencies? How and when are they acquired?

Can they easily be taught? Are there systematic (for example gender) differences in these competencies? How are they measured? Are people accurate at self-assessment? Are they linked in any systematic way, that is, is there an underlying structure to these beliefs? And, most importantly, what is their relationship to cognitive ability as measured by conventional power tests of intelligence? It seems now that to attract attention the word intelligence is put after any skill or competency to give it respectability.

Yet more quotients of "intelligence"

Eichinger and Lombardo (2004) identified both what they call the "Six Qs of Leadership" and an explanation for how they combined to lead to success or failure. They note how important leadership is to business success. Thus comparing the top with the bottom 10 per cent and the effect on a company's bottom line shows a staggering $5 million (£2.5 million) difference.

But many executives, they argue, fail through lack of accountability, initiative and openness to new ideas, social skills and the ability to learn from mistakes. They tend to be content to use old, familiar, approaches to problems. They underestimate problems and are very concerned with both their image/reputation and that of the company. Indeed they see their interests as totally intertwined with those of the company. They are intolerant of disagreement, self-centered and narrow. They neither inspire others nor deliver results.

For many failed leaders derailment comes as a shock to both themselves and their companies because of their own success. Creativity turns into just being disorganized chaos, assertiveness turns into aggression, action orientation changes into lack of planning success. Early success has made them overconfident and too rooted in past behaviors. They may also be too self-reliant and unable to build teams and maintain productive relationships with others.

For Eichinger and Lombardo (2004) the Qs are:

1. *Intelligence quotient (IQ)* – Information processing, a good memory and ability to learn; the definition of IQ. It's very important and easy to assess. Managers who can handle large amounts of information, see patterns and trends, and multitask do best. Amen.
2. *Technical/operational quotient (TQ)* – It measures how able managers are to manage ideas and projects, understand salient technology

and operations and, in short, get things done. Those who fail may be too dependent on a single competency or poor at initializing or following through. Again it's easy to assess by on-the-job measures of success. It is therefore particularly important early on in a career.

3. *Motivational quotient (MQ)* – This is the desire to achieve, lead and succeed and be prepared to sacrifice quality of life and work-life balance for it. It is about perseverance, getting results and a focused compulsion to master the tasks at hand. It's about energy, commitment and goal-setting. The high-MQ manager pursues stretching goals, which get them out of their comfort zone.

4. *Experience quotient (XQ)* – This refers to the amount and kinds (quantity and quality) of experiences managers have had. Some experiences are more "developmental" than others. They learn more from personal experience than from the stories of others and they can be taught to benefit from experience. So, working abroad, making changes in scope, size and area, and starting something from scratch are all relevant. It's about dealing with hardships and setbacks. Some bosses help by giving their staff wide experience of different problem domains. More is better, breadth is better.

5. *People quotient (PQ)* – This is about self-management and self-awareness of motives, emotions and actions and their effect on subsequent behavior and others. Next there is a curiosity and openness with others. This is the essential, inspirational, charming stuff. Building strong bonds, strong teams, keeping the troops happy, being open and sensitive to others. Those with low PQ don't, can't or won't appropriately delegate or empower others. It is working with and through others, not moving away from or against them. Low PQ means poor, shallow relationships. It's really EQ relabeled.

6. *Learning quotient (LQ)* – This is soft learning – to think, manage and solve problems in a different way. It's "street smarts." People with higher LQ cope better with ambiguity and complexity; they experiment and handle new ideas deftly. They are characterized by curiosity and imagination. They seize opportunities and adapt well to new situations. They learn to adapt and hence survive. "Know-it-alls," who resist feedback and don't share knowledge, fail. This skill is best tested in new assignments, ventures, mergers and acquisitions and responding to new competitors. Learning agility is good. It is the ability to make the most of experience.

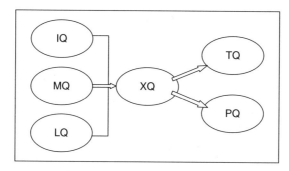

Figure I.1   The relationship between six types of "intelligence"

Note that these authors talk of quotients, not "intelligences." That is they are measurable but not necessarily to be thought of as intelligence.

Another way to look at the 6Q model (Figure I.1) is that the basic raw ingredients of success are sufficient IQ and MQ – smart and motivated enough – along with sufficient LQ to learn from experience (XQ). Assuming that the experiences are relevant and powerful enough, people should be able to learn the TQ and PQ skills (but not the personality part) necessary for success – which involves getting significant work done with and through others.

So what would be our recommendation to build leaders who will endure like architectural masterpieces?

Our blueprint includes the following seven components:

1. Educate managers and executives about the existence, and contributions, of all six quotients on the building blocks for long-lasting success.
2. Work to de-emphasize the focus on IQ, TQ and MQ. Although these may be easy to assess and are likely to be correlated with performance up through the managerial ranks, they are not the distinguishing characteristics of those who succeed over time at the executive level.
3. Instead, put more emphasis on LQ, XQ and PQ throughout employees' careers. Integrate these values solidly into the culture and ensure that the recognition and reward systems are aligned.
4. Systematically assess LQ much earlier in people's organizational tenure so that more realistic high-potential designations and more meaningful career paths can be developed.

5. Allocate resources to enhance LQ for those who score in the top third, or even half, of the possible range, so that they are fully equipped to learn the lessons ensconced in all the experiences and challenges they encounter.

6. Focus on the aspects of PQ that enhance or doom careers – encourage an acceptable interpersonal style and neutralize dysfunctional personality patterns.

7. Understand that with XQ, you can't learn from experiences you're not having. Variety of experience gives the opportunity to gain breadth of skills.

Emotional intelligence

Of all the "hot" intelligences it was, and is, however the idea of *emotional intelligence* that has most captivated people's imagination. Just as history is told by the victors so the story of EI is told rather differently by different groups. Some claim EI was part of the "multiple-intelligence" movement dating back to the social intelligences of the 1920s (Petrides *et al.* 2004) or the mischievous muddling of McClelland responsible for other similar concepts like competency.

Goleman's international bestseller (1995) and follow-up (1998) propelled EI into the limelight and influenced most subsequent conceptualizations of EI. Towards the latter half of the 1990s, the first EI measures started to appear.

A difficulty arises however with deciding exactly which are the "facets" or components of EI. As Petrides and Furnham (2001: 428) put it, "asking what precisely should be part of a construct is like asking what sports should be in the Olympics; neither questions can be answered objectively." Petrides *et al.* (2004) have however listed facets of EQ that appear in different conceptualizations of the concept (Table I.3).

However, Perez *et al.* (2005) have found eight other models of different dimensions of EI, showing there is still much disagreement in the area (Table I.4).

There now exist a large number of measures of EI, many of which are poorly constructed and validated. Perez *et al.* (2005) in an exhaustive review found, described and evaluated 5 ability EQ tests and 15 trait measures.

Petrides *et al.* (2004) argue that trait EI encompasses behavioral tendencies and *self-perceived* abilities, as opposed to *actual* cognitive abilities;

Table I.3   Common facets in salient models of EI

Facets	High scorers perceive themselves as . . .
Adaptability	Flexible and willing to adapt to new conditions.
Assertiveness	Forthright, frank, and willing to stand up for their rights.
Emotional expression	Capable of communicating their feelings to others.
Emotional management (others)	Capable of influencing others people's feelings.
Emotional perception (self and others)	Clear about their own and other people's feelings.
Emotional regulation	Capable of controlling their emotions.
Impulsiveness (low)	Reflective and less likely to give in to their urges.
Relationship skills	Capable of having fulfilling personal relationships.
Self-esteem	Successful and self-confident.
Self-motivation	Driven and unlikely to give up in the face of adversity.
Social competence	Accomplished in networking with excellent social skills.
Stress management	Capable of withstanding pressure and regulating stress.
Trait empathy	Capable of taking someone else's perspective.
Trait happiness	Cheerful and satisfied with their lives.
Trait optimism	Confident and likely to "look on the bright side" of life.

it belongs in the realm of personality. In contrast, ability EI, which encompasses actual abilities, belongs primarily in the domain of cognitive ability. While trait EI is hypothesized to be orthogonal to cognitive ability, EI should be related mainly to general intelligence (g), but also to specific personality dimensions that reflect basic individual differences in emotionality (especially neuroticism).

Traditionally psychologists have argued and demonstrated that personality and intelligence are effectively unrelated to one another. It seems that normal dimensions of personality are essentially not related to ability tests even when the former are measured by objective tests. Yet recent models have attempted to integrate these two basic dimensions of differential psychology.

What of the layperson? Many talk of EQ as a skill, some of it being like intuition. Laypeople seem as divided on the issue as the academics. However, commercially the trait camp has won. There are dozens of poor or non-psychometrized instruments on the market. A web search soon confirms this. Nearly all are questionnaires: self-report measures that have high face validity, and possibly high fakability. They look like older measures of assertiveness, social skill or interpersonal style. Ability measures are difficult to devise and take time to administer. Also they may not always appear to be relevant to people in business who may be interested in training EQ or selecting those with high scores.

Table I.4   Summary of EI models

Salovey and Mayer (1990)	• Appraisal and expression of emotion • Utilization of emotion • Regulation of emotion	
Goleman (1995)	• Self-awareness • Self-regulation • Self-motivation • Empathy • Handling relationships	
Mayer and Salovey (1997)	• Perception, appraisal, and expression of emotion • Emotional facilitation of thinking • Understanding and analysing emotions; employing emotional knowledge • Reflective regulation of emotions to promote emotional and intellectual growth	
Bar-On (1997)	**Intrapersonal** • Emotional self-awareness • Assertiveness • Self-regard • Self-actualization • Independence **Interpersonal** • Empathy • Interpersonal relationships • Social responsibility **General** • Happiness • Optimism	**Adaptation** • Problem-solving • Reality-testing • Flexibility **Stress management** • Stress tolerance • Impulse control
Cooper and Sawaf (1997)	**Emotional literacy** • Emotional fitness • Emotional depth • Emotional alchemy	
Goleman (1998)	**Self-awareness** • Emotional self-awareness • Accurate self-assessment • Self-confidence **Self-regulation** • Self-control • Trustworthiness • Conscientiousness • Adaptability • Innovation **Self-motivation** • Achievement orientation • Commitment • Initiative • Optimism	**Empathy** • Empathy • Organizational awareness • Service orientation • Developing others • Leveraging diversity **Social skills** • Leadership • Communication • Influence • Change catalysis • Conflict management • Building bonds • Collaboration and co-operation • Team capabilities

(Continued)

Table I.4   (Continued)

Weisinger (1998)	**Self-awareness**
	• Emotional management
	• Self-motivation
	• Effective communication skills
	• Interpersonal expertise
	• Emotional coaching
Higgs and Dulewicz (1999)	**Drivers**
	• Motivation
	• Intuitiveness
	Constrainers
	• Conscientiousness
	• Emotional resilience
	Enablers
	• Self-awareness
	• Interpersonal sensitivity
	• Influence
	• Trait

Laypeople, even hardheaded business people, are surprisingly unimpressed by psychometric evidence, or, worse, uninterested in it. Because they do not either understand or care about concepts like test–retest reliability, Cronbach's alpha, predictive validity or orthogonal dimensionality, they appear to buy questionnaire products on packaging and promise much more than on evidence. This partly explains the popularity of EI. Demand is quickly met by supply, but not by many reputable test-publishers because validation is too time-consuming. This does not however prevent others from aggressively marketing their essentially "not proven" products. (The number of instruments around can itself even promote enthusiasm for these products, as it may make them appear more popular than they are.)

Emotional intelligence at work

It was no doubt Goleman's book that electrified the public and popularized the term. He has retried to capture attention more recently with "social intelligence" (Goleman 2006). In his 1998 book he extended his ideas to the workplace. He now has over 25 facets, subsumed under 5 domains. Anyone inspecting this system (see below) would be astounded by the conceptual muddle at both levels. Thus personality traits, like conscientiousness, are subsumed under the domain of self-regulation. Equally unrelated psychological concepts like initiative and optimism are classified under motivation. It seems difficult, in fact, to say what is not a facet of EQ. That is: does it have any divergent validity?

The emotional intelligences at work

Personal competence – competencies that determine how we manage ourselves

Self-awareness – *knowing one's internal states, preferences, resources and institutions*

- **Emotional awareness** – recognizing emotions and their effects.
- **Accurate self-assessment** – knowing own strengths and limits.
- **Self-confidence** – strong sense of self-worth and capabilities.

Self-regulation – *managing one's internal states, impulses and resources*

- **Self-control** – keeping disruptive emotions and impulses in check.
- **Trustworthiness** – maintaining standards of honesty and integrity.
- **Conscientiousness** – taking responsibility for personal performance.
- **Adaptability** – flexibility in handling change.
- **Innovation** – being comfortable with novel ideas, approaches and new information.

Motivation – *emotional tendencies that guide or facilitate reaching goals*

- **Achievement drive** – striving to improve or meet a standard of excellence.
- **Commitment** – aligning with the goals of the group or organization.
- **Initiative** – readiness to act on opportunities.
- **Optimism** – persistence in pursuing goals despite obstacles or setbacks.

Personal competence – competencies that determine how we manage relationships

Empathy – *awareness of others' feelings, needs and concerns*

- **Understanding others** – sensing others' feelings and perspectives and taking an active interest in their concerns.
- **Developing others** – sensing others' development needs and bolstering their abilities.

- **Service orientation** – anticipating, recognising and meeting customer needs.
- **Leveraging diversity** – cultivating opportunities through different kinds of people.
- **Political awareness** – reading a group's emotional currents and power relationships.

Social skills – *adeptness at inducing desirable responses in others*
- **Influence** – wielding effective tactics for persuasion.
- **Communication** – listening openly and sending convincing messages.
- **Conflict management** – negotiating and resolving disagreements.
- **Leadership** – inspiring and guiding individuals and groups.
- **Change catalyst** – initiating or managing change.
- **Building bonds** – nurturing instrumental relationships.
- **Collaboration and cooperation** – working with others toward shared goals.
- **Team capabilities** – creating group synergy in pursuing collective goals.

Goleman argues (usually without good, direct evidence) that, at work, relationship building is more important than technical skills. Further, he reasons that technical training, in the essential job knowledge of any career, from accounting to zoology, is easy compared with teaching EQ skills. That is, as an adult it is comparatively more straightforward to learn the technical aspects of the job than the soft skills. The idea seems to be that there is a critical period to acquire the bases of EI, which is probably during early to late adolescence. The young person, often a male, may experience social anxiety, discomfort and rejection while attempting to interact with and influence others (in particular those they are attracted to, which is most often people of the opposite sex).

Hence they may over time find solace in computers and other activities with a high-skills–low-contact basis. Thus, in early adulthood, they appear to be technically very competent in certain areas (IT, engineering) but still rather undeveloped in people skills and especially emotional awareness and regulation. They may even be "phobic" about emotional issues and resistant to (social skills) training. It is also assumed that people are less able to pick up EI "skills" as well as less willing to try. To acquire technical skills often requires considerable dedication, and opportunities to acquire social skills (EQ) are, therefore, reduced.

Then the low-EQ person chooses technology rather than people for fun, comfort and a source of ideas because they do not understand emotions.

The argument goes, according to Goleman, that failed and derailed managers tend to be rigid, with poor self-control and poor social skills, and weak at building bonds. And yet understanding and using emotions/feelings are at the heart of business and indeed of being human. It is, says Goleman (1998), no accident that *motive* and *emotion* share the same Latin root, meaning to move – great work starts with great feeling.

But the book seems to have an over-inclusive view of what EQ is. There are lists of facets and features, some derivative of each other, some quite unrelated to anything about emotion (see pp. 16–17). It does echo themes in the zeitgeist – hence its popularity. The book is also easy to dip into, with many summaries and précis. Hence, there were, and indeed still are, a rash of magazine and newspaper articles that popularized the book and the concept. This is not "trickle-down" economics but a waterfall of publicity. The sheer amount of positive publicity given to the book must be one of the factors involved in its success and the popularity of the concept at the heart of it.

In his 1995 book Goleman claimed that cognitive ability (i.e. intelligence) contributed around 20 per cent toward life success but that the remaining 80 per cent is directly attributable to emotional intelligence. In a later book (1998) he lists 25 social competencies from conflict management to self-control, all of which make up social competencies that lead to success at work.

Equally in their book *Executive EQ*, Cooper and Sawaf (1997) put forth the four cornerstones of emotional intelligence at the executive level: *emotional literacy* (involves the knowledge and understanding of one's own emotions and how they function), *emotional fitness* (involves trustworthiness and emotional hardiness and flexibility), *emotional depth* (involves emotional growth and intensity) and *emotional alchemy* (involves using emotions to discover creative opportunities).

More recently Zeidner *et al.* (2004) provided a useful critical overview of the role of EQ in the workplace. As they note, business people prefer often to talk about emotional competencies, rather than traits or abilities – competencies being essentially learned capabilities. In this sense, EQ is "the potential to become skilled at learning certain emotional responses" (p. 377). It therefore does not ensure that individuals *will* (as opposed to *can*) manifest competent behaviors at work. Thus, EQ is an index of potential. However, emotional competence does, it is argued, assist in learning (soft) interpersonal skills.

Zeidner *et al.* (2004) tried to specify these emotional competencies. They include: emotional self-awareness, emotional self-regulation, social-emotional awareness, regulating emotions in others, understanding emotions and so on. If one is to include older, related, concepts like social skills or interpersonal competencies then it is possible to find a literature dating back thirty years, showing that these skills predict occupational effectiveness and success. Further, there is convincing empirical literature which suggests that these skills can be improved and learnt.

However Zeidner *et al.* (2004) are quite rightly eager to squash the IQ-vs.-EQ myth. They note (my italics):

> [*S*]*everal unsubstantiated claims* have appeared in the popular literature and the media about the significance of EI in the workplace. Thus, EI has been claimed to validly predict a variety of successful behaviors at work, at a level exceeding that of intelligence . . . Of note, however, Goleman is unable to cite empirical data supporting any causal link between EI and any of its supposed, positive effects. (p. 380)

The authors quite rightly point out that EQ measures must demonstrate criterion, discriminant, incremental and predictive validity to be cost effective in business and scientifically sound. We know that general ability (*g*) predicts around 20 to 30 per cent of the variance in (higher) job performance across all jobs, all criteria, but more for complex jobs.

They review studies which provide positive, mixed and negative results. Quite rightly they offer critiques of the studies which purport to show EQ linked to work success. Typical problems include:

- The psychometric properties of the EQ measure.
- Not controlling for intelligence (cognitive ability) or personality factors.
- Not having very robust measures of work-related behavior.
- Not being able to disentangle the direction of causality through using longitudinal studies.
- Having too many impressionistic, anecdotal studies and too few published in peer review journals.

The authors are also interested in the explanation for the process. Thus *if* EQ does predict satisfaction, productivity, teamwork and so on then the question is: what is the *process* or *mechanism* that accounts for this? It seems from the literature that there are various speculations to account for this:

- High-EQ people are better at communicating their ideas, intentions and goals. They are more articulate, assertive and sensitive.
- EQ is closely associated with teamwork social skills, which are very important at work.
- Business leaders, high in EQ, build supportive climates, which increase organizational commitment, which in turn leads to success.
- High-EQ leaders are perceptive and know their own and their teams' strengths and weaknesses, which enable them to leverage the former and compensate for the latter.
- EQ is related to effective and efficient coping skills, which enable people to deal better with demands, pressure and stress.
- High-EQ leaders can identify accurately what followers feel and need, as well as being more inspiring and supportive. They generate more excitement, enthusiasm and optimism.
- High-EQ managers, unlike their low-EQ companions, are less prone to negative, defensive and destructive coping and decision-making styles.

Zeidner *et al.* (2004) end with an evaluative summary and guidelines for doing good research in the area:

> Overall, this section of our review suggests that the current excitement surrounding the potential benefits from the use of EI in the workplace may be premature or even misplaced. Whereas EI appears related to performance and affective outcomes, the evidence for performance is very limited and often contradictory. Much of the predictive validity of questionnaire measures of EI may be a product of their overlap with standard personality factors. Furthermore, the literature is replete with unsubstantiated generalizations, with much of the existing evidence bearing on the role of EI in occupational success either anecdotal or impressionistic and/or based on unpublished or in-house research. Thus, a number of basic questions still loom large: Do emotionally intelligent employees produce greater profits for the organization? Does EI enhance wellbeing at the workplace? Are the effects of training in EI likely to result in increases in job performance and/or work satisfaction? (p. 380)

In order to provide both good theory and evidence to support the use of EQ in organizational settings, Zeidner *et al.* (2004) recommend the following:

- The measure of EQ used needs to have reliability and validity and be clearly differentiated from related constructs: "A science of EI requires specifying the definition, number, type and range of primary emotional abilities within a formal psychometric model" (p. 390).
- Researchers need to match the test to the job and specify precisely the context and process by which it works. They recommend an emotional task analysis to understand how EQ works in different jobs.
- Researchers need good measures of the criterion job behavior; they need to look at facets or components of EQ, and they need to measure other variables like IQ or personality traits.

And their final conclusion is this:

> Despite the important role attributed to a wide array of emotional competencies in the workplace, there is currently only a modicum of research supporting the meaningful role attributed to EI (and nested emotional competencies) in determining occupational success. Many of the popular claims presented in the literature regarding the role of EI in determining work success and well-being are rather misleading in that they seem to present scientific studies supporting their claims, while in fact failing to do so. In short, despite some rather fantastic claims to the contrary, the guiding principle appears presently as "caveat emptor." (p. 393)

Management fads

The application of EI in the workplace seems the virtual prototype of a fad. Furnham (2006) suggested that all management fads have a similar natural history, which has seven separate identifiable phases. One question is whether EQ will follow this trajectory and, if so, where is it now?

1. *Academic discovery* – Faddish ideas can often be traced to the distinctly unfaddish world of academia. A modest discovery may result in a pretty indigestible paper in a specialist journal. These papers show the causal link between two factors relevant to work situations. Such works are not

only dry, complicated and heavily statistical; they are also cautious and preliminary. Academics often call for replications and more research, are hesitant and underline the complexity of all the actual and possible factors involved. Few are interested in immediate application. Their job is understanding the process, not changing the world. The early social and emotional intelligence papers are a little like this. However, it is difficult to trace the concept to one study or paper.

2. *Description of the study* – This process can last a long time, and usually involves a lot of elaboration and distortion along the way. Someone reads the paper and provides a summary. The summary may be verbal and if so may end a little like Chinese whispers. Others hear it and repeat it, but with each repetition the findings become stronger and the complexity weaker. In this sense effect-size estimates go up and criticisms about experimental technique go down. Selective memory ensures that the crucial findings are recorded and embellished. At this stage, it is unlikely that the researchers would recognise the findings as they were in the first place. This phase is difficult to document, but it is often trainers, consultants and industrial/organizational psychologists who are primarily responsible for this phase.

3. *Popularization in a bestseller* – The next stage is for a business writer/guru to take up the call. He/she hears about the findings and gives them a catchy title – before you know what the fad is about to begin. That one single and simple idea/finding/process soon becomes a book. This is where the Goleman (1998) book plays such an important role. It was widely reviewed in the media around the world. Quizzes began to appear and it soon entered both common consciousness and the language. When there is a bestseller with a snappy title and publisher hype, the average manager at least reads a few reviews of the book. He or she may even buy it, but many are content to get the gist from reviewers. They are frequently envious of seemingly powerful results that occur when the great idea is followed. It is at this stage that the fad becomes a buzzword.

4. *Consultant hype and universalization* – It is not the academic or the author that really powers the fad but an army of management consultants trying to look as if they are at the cutting edge of management theory. Because the concepts are easy to understand and are said to have wide application, the consultants seek to apply them everywhere. Those who don't climb aboard are made to feel left out, "fuddy-duddy," even bad for their shareholders. What made the EQ phenomenon different were

two things. The first was the web, which now has a very big impact on the rapid and universal popularization of ideas. The second factor was the rapid development of measures of EQ. The concept not only struck home, but was (supposedly) very easy to measure efficiently and validly. It was the measurement of EQ that really appealed to the management consultants.

5. *Total commitment by true believers* – At this point, the evangelism moves from the consultant to the managers. For a small number of companies, the technique *seems* to have brought quick, massive benefits. They become happy and willing product champions, which only serves to sell more books and fan the fires of faddishness. EQ champions are paraded at conferences. EQ awareness, courses and training improve performance and make people into better managers. The total quality management (TQM) movement seems an excellent exemplar of the process.

   With hindsight, it is sometimes difficult to explain why the concept had such an impact on the lay public or why people seem to believe it worked. This is somewhere between the Hawthorne effect and the placebo effect. The former refers to the way people react positively when they are treated differently (irrespective of what the treatment consists of) while the latter refers to the sugar pill effect, where simply believing that it will do you good is enough.

   In fact, years after the fad has passed, there are little outstations of believers who continue to be the faithful. In time, they are quiet reminders of the past as they cling on. The Amish of management, they resolutely hang on to their old ways.

6. *Doubt, scepticism and defection* – After pride comes the fall. After a few years of heavy product-selling, the appetite for the fad becomes diminished. The market is saturated. Various "new and improved" or just as likely "shorter and simpler" versions of the fad are introduced. But it is apparent that the enthusiasm is gone. And then the avalanche or mudslide begins. It begins with managerial doubt and then academic skepticism, followed by journalistic cynicism and finally consultant defection. It may be that the whole process starts with people pointing out the poor cost–benefit analysis of introducing the fad. Or it may occur because someone goes back to the original finding and shows that the gap has widened so much between what was initially demonstrated and what is now done that the two are different species.

Then management journalists smell blood. It is easy to find disaffected managers happy to squeal. They point out the thousands spent for little reward and what an incredible consultant ripoff the whole thing has become. A trickle becomes a stream and then a river. And the consultants who were so eager to pick up the fad are the first to drop it. What gave them both credibility and massive "invoiceability" now makes them look like con-artists as they distance themselves from the fad. But this phase may be some time away with EQ. After all the fad, at least in marketplace terms, is only five to ten years old. No alternative is on the horizon. Many organizations are still in the early part of their infatuation with the idea. But nemesis may be not too far behind.

7. *New discoveries* – The end of one fad is an ideal time for trainers, writers and consultants to spot a gap in the market. They know there is an incurable thirst for magic-bullet, fix-all solutions, so the whole process starts again. The really clever people begin to sense when the previous fad is reaching its sell-by date, so that they have just enough time to write their new bestseller to get the market exactly right.

Is EI a management or educational fad? Has it passed through the above phases? And if so where is it now? Certainly the academics are only now beginning to respond with careful, considered research that attempts to unpick the concept. Suddenly the academic journals particularly in differential psychology are bursting with papers that take (hopefully) a disinterested scientific and measured look at EI (Austin 2004). There has also appeared a serious, thoughtful and balanced review of work in the area to date (Matthews *et al.* 2002). Academic researchers are not immune to fad and fashion. However the lag time is longer and thus what interests the two worlds of science and practice may easily be out of sync.

This book

There is no doubt that social skills, social intelligence and the emotional sensitivity of managers at work are very important. Emotional perceptiveness, sensitivity and management are more important in some jobs rather than others. More than twenty years ago after a study of airline cabin staff, Hochschild (1983) wrote a book, *The Managed Heart: Commercialization of Human Feeling*. In it she argued for a new concept: *emotional labour*.

She said many jobs required physical and mental labour but some, uniquely, required emotional labor.

The idea is that service staff are required to express emotions they do not necessarily feel. They are required to smile, be positive and appear relaxed whatever they are actually experiencing. Hochschild called this *surface acting*. However, in some jobs you are almost required to feel these emotions. This is called *deep acting*. The idea is that (canny) customers can spot the false display of emotion so you have to learn the "inside-out smile."

Service staff have to learn to become method actors. Karl Marx said workers were alienated from the products of their labor. Equally, Hochschild believed service workers, whose emotions are "managed and controlled" by their employers, become alienated from their real feelings. Hochschild argued that this cost too much, in that it caused psychological damage in the long term. Yet there remains controversy, not so much about the concept but whether it is essentially damaging in the way it alienates workers from their true feelings. This book is about much more than the social intelligences. The essays take a wider perspective. But there remains no doubt that intelligence and social skills are fundamental requisites for managerial success.

References

Austin, E. (2004) "An Investigation of the Relationship between Trait Emotional Intelligence and Emotional Task Performance," *Personality and Individual Differences, 36*, 1855–64.

Bar-On, R. (1997) *BarOn Emotional Quotient Inventory (EQ-i): Technical Manual.* Toronto: Multi-Health Systems.

Conrad, S. and Milburn, M. (2001) *Sexual Intelligence.* New York: Crown.

Cooper, R. K. and Sawaf, A. (1997) *Executive EQ: Emotional Intelligence in Leadership and Organizations.* New York: Grosset, Putnam.

Eichinger, R. and Lombardo, M. (2004) "The 6 Qs of Leadership. A Blueprint for Enduring Success at the Top." Unpublished.

Emmons, R. (2000) "Is Spirituality an Intelligence?," *International Journal for the Psychology of Religion, 10*, 3–26.

Furnham, A. (2005) "Gender and Personality Difference in Self and Other Ratings of Business Intelligence," *British Journal of Management, 16*, 91–103.

Furnham, A. (2006) "Explaining the Popularity of Emotional Intelligence," in K. Murphy (ed.) *A Critique of Emotional Intelligence.* New York: LEA, 141–59.

Gardner, J. (1983) *Frames of Mind: The Theory of Multiple Intelligences.* New York: Basic Books.

Gardner, J. (1999) *Intelligence Reframed: Multiple Intelligence for the 21st Century.* New York: Basic Books.

Goleman, D. (1995) *Emotional Intelligence: Why It Can Matter More Than IQ.* New York: Bantam.

Goleman, D. (1998) *Working with Emotional Intelligence.* New York: Bantam.

Goleman, D. (2006) *Social Intelligence: The New Science of Human Relationships.* New York: Bantam.

Gottfredson, L. (2003) "Dissecting Practical Intelligence Theory," *Intelligence, 31,* 343–97.

Harvey, M., Novicevic, M. and Kiessling, T. (2002) "Development of Multiple IQ Maps for the Use in the Selection of Impatriate Managers: A Practical Theory," *International Journal of Intercultural Relations, 26,* 493–524.

Higgs, M. J. and Dulewicz, S. V. (1999) *Making Sense of Emotional Intelligence.* Windsor: NFER-Nelson.

Hochschild, A. (1983) *The Managed Heart: Commercialization of Human Feeling.* Berkeley: University of California Press.

Mackintosh, N. (1998) *IQ and Human Intelligence.* Oxford University Press.

Mayer, J. D. and Salovey, P. (1997) "What Is Emotional Intelligence?," in P. Salovey and D. J. Sluyter (eds) *Emotional Development and Emotional Intelligence: Educational Implications.* New York: Basic Books, 3–31.

Perez, J., Petrides, K. V. and Furnham, A. (2005) "Measuring Trait Emotional Intelligence," in R. Schulze and R. Roberts (eds) *Emotional Intelligence: An International Handbook.* Gottingen: Hogrefe, 181–201.

Petrides, K. V., Frederickson, N. and Furnham, A. (2004) "The Role of Trait Emotional Intelligence in Academic Performance and Deviant Behaviour at School," *Personality and Individual Differences, 36,* 277–93.

Petrides, K. V. and Furnham, A. (2001) "Trait Emotional Intelligence," *European Journal of Personality, 15,* 425–48.

Petrides, K. V., Furnham, A. and Frederickson, N. (2004) "Emotional Intelligence," *Psychologist, 17,* 574–7.

Riggio, R., Murphy, S. and Pirozzolo, F. (2002) *Multiple Intelligences and Leadership.* London: Erlbaum.

Salovey, P. and Mayer, J. D. (1990) "Emotional Intelligence," *Imagination, Cognition and Personality, 9,* 185–211.

Sternberg, R. (1985) *Beyond IQ: A Triarchic Theory of Human Intelligence.* New York: Cambridge University Press.

Sternberg, R. (1997) *Successful Intelligence.* New York: Plume.

Visser, B., Ashton, M. and Vernon, P. (2006) "Beyond *g*: Putting Multiple Intelligences Theory to the Test," *Intelligence, 34,* 487–502.

Zeidner, M., Matthews, G. and Roberts, R. (2004) "Emotional Intelligence in the Workplace: A Critical Review," *Applied Psychology, 33,* 371–99.

Affirmative shopping

What is the difference between affirmative shopping, distributive justice, and Robin Hood ethics? At the heart of the notion of "robbing the rich to pay the poor" are the concepts of fairness and natural justice.

So when an unemployed and uneducated Third World person steals goods from a highly successful multinational grocery store some are willing to tag this in a humorous and forgiving way as "affirmative shopping." And when the hotel staff steal your toiletries as opposed to you liberating the soap and shower cap you can be sanguine and tolerant or outraged by criminal behavior.

Such dilemmas are now the stuff of the intriguing world of business ethics. But ethics is plural. One can adopt an ethical code, but would be unwise to assume there is only one. Thus when self-righteous, self-serving and self-important firms trumpet their ethical stance on some issues they seem to imply that if you do differently you are unethical.

This is not to assert anything-goes relativism. It is however to suggest that different ethical codes can be applied to the same conditions but yield different answers. Thus good Christians can be both pro and anti abortion, mercy-killing and capital punishment; be homophilic or phobic. All believe they are morally and ethically right and have Biblical texts and well-rehearsed arguments in support of their positions.

But the issue for the busy manager is what to do about staff pilfering, or whether to have a "shoplifting policy." First question: should one differentiate between the two? Theft is theft. So there are those who advocate the "zero-tolerance" code. All incidents are treated the same. No matter who the "criminal" or what the size/value/importance of the item "liberated," the policy will be the same: call the police, sack the employee.

This black-and-white world however makes some very costly assumptions. First, that it is easy to prove the clear criminality of the "alternative shopper." Most will dispute the crime: it was not intentional or quite simply the facts are wrong. Very soon lawyers are involved – lawyers from both sides, of course.

There needs to be evidence and documentation. This involves people and time, which equals dough. Some believe a cost-effective solution is videocameras: the ubiquitous surveillance camera. But is that allowable evidence? And at what cost are they installed and people found to monitor them?

The zero-tolerance, go-to-court approach soon becomes expensive. An object worth £3.00 which retails at £10.00 is allegedly stolen. The cost of getting a conviction may be easily 100 times that. Worth it perhaps if (and only if) it can be clearly shown really to deter people from doing this in the future. But where's the evidence?

And that is about enough to prompt a change of policy – and with it a change in ethics. This can be a bit tricky. Why is stealing something small different from something big?

One answer lies in the demography and motive of the accused. What about the little old lady who "forgets" to pay? What of the down-and-out who is genuinely hungry? Are they easily distinguishable from the habitual thief?

And what about staff pilfering? Are they badly paid, badly managed people sensitive to, and deeply envious, of the enormous difference between their "pay and rations" and those of the chap at the top? Worse, do supervisors turn a blind eye to the disappearance of certain goods (often from the kitchen) because either they sympathize with those under them, or worse, it is the only lever they have to reward staff? Think of the implications of sacking those caught stealing if this is true.

Pay people well, pay them market rate, treat them well and alternative, affirmative, in-house shopping decreases. It never goes away completely because there are always those with a slack moral code happy to exploit any opportunistic situation. Management sensitivity and reward equity are cheaper in both the long and the short run compared with introducing cameras and other security measures.

But what about light-fingered customers? That's not so easy. Contest only cases you think you might win? Not exactly a clear moral code there. Try to name-and-shame a few to act as a deterrent? Turn a blind eye to most cases while still having a sensible policy to ensure it is not easy to do this sort of "shopping"?

Ethics is a minefield. That's why people use committees to diffuse responsibility. But internal and external theft is also an economic issue. Big grocery stores lose well over one hundred million pounds a year from stock shrinkage and shoplifting. So it is important to think about what to do.

One thing is certain. Making light of it by neologisms solves nothing. Affirmative shopping is theft.

All chiefs now

In his famous hierarchy of needs the humanistic psychologist Abraham Maslow argued that to explore and exploit our talents fully through the process of self-actualization, we have to have our more basic needs satisfied first.

Most people alas are "born to waste their fragrance on the desert air" because they struggle with an insufficiently fulfilled need: self-esteem. Indeed there has been a whole, and now thankfully discredited, movement that saw self-esteem enhancement as the solution to nearly all the world's problems. Delinquents would reform; the seemingly uneducable would pass with flying colors; the meek would inherit the earth. All through a self-esteem boost.

Make people feel good about themselves and they would (miraculously) perform better. It's the stuff of sport psychology. And of course mostly nonsense. Self-esteem follows from success: it does not cause it. Teach people skills, play to their abilities, coach them and they perform – and then feel better about themselves.

The business community appears to have swallowed the self-esteem guff hook, line and sinker. Or perhaps they have been pressurized by narcissistic staff. The most dramatic illustration of this is job titles. Despite the fact that it has been fashionable to flatten organizations (in both senses) there seems to be a serious inflation in job titles.

In the old days the top guy was simply called the CEO. One chief, many Indians. People who reported to the CEO were usually called directors and they were "on the board." Now they prefer to be chiefs themselves so we have:

1. *Chief Administrative Officer*. Typists became secretaries became PAs. Never underestimate their power and importance. Keeping them sweet is all important.
2. *Chief Communications Officer*. This used to be the switchboard personnel, but now big organizations have an entire PR department staffed compulsorily by girls called Amanda and Caroline. They are the charming face of the whole organization.

3. *Chief Ethics Officer.* This is a new post. We have ethical investments and products and processes and systems. No one quite knows what these are but we all know it's important and a good thing. The CEthO sorts it out.

4. *Chief Facilities Officer.* The maintenance department needs a head to raise its profile. Someone has to buy the office chairs. Someone has to pop round with ladder and toolbox when the blinds don't work, the door doesn't shut or the lights are flickering. They all report to the CFasO.

5. *Chief Horticultural Officer.* Some organizations have pretty gardens; beautifully landscaped verges and plots to delight the eye. Teams of gardeners labor all year to curb mother nature. They report to the CHO who is often a real enthusiast.

6. *Chief Hygiene Officer.* Never underestimate the importance of the cleansing department and that army of (migrant worker) cleaning staff who labor after lights out or at dawn in the office. Their boss has to become the CHO.

7. *Chief Litigation Officer.* The Health and Safety department have a bad name with their ridiculous, overcautious, litigation-phobic behavior. So they need rebranding. Desperately and quickly. And nothing is better than a semi-frightening, legal word. So welcome the CLO whose job, of course, is to prevent litigation against the organization, while perhaps enthusiastically prosecuting it against others.

8. *Chief Nocturnal Officer.* Some organizations work around the clock. Someone is "in charge" in the "wee small hours." Not an MBA strategist nor a charming PR type executive, he or she remains crucial for the business.

9. *Chief Nourishment Officer.* An organization, like an army, marches on its stomach. Never underestimate the restorative power of a good lunch. Never assume the canteen is pure overhead. It is the source of wellbeing and nourishment. Hence the need for a CNO.

10. *Chief Receiving Officer.* Consultants will tell you that you can gauge the corporate culture and values of an organization when you walk into reception. The layout and facilities are important, but so is the way you are greeted and processed. Surely all organizations require a competent CRO.

11. *Chief Security Officer.* Security everywhere has been taken more seriously. It has been suggested that Osama Bin Laden bought shares in security firms to pay for his outrages. One needs to be secure from

thieves, from spies, from competitors and from saboteurs. We certainly need a well-trained, hypervigilant, even slightly paranoid CSO.

There are other positions one could dream up. This trend is ubiquitous. Small, dreary town councils fancy themselves as "cabinets". Head of Street Cleansing is a Health Minister. There was a time when you knew who really was the boss. Now to feed the insatiable vanity of the modern worker, we certainly have too many chiefs and not enough Indians.

Anti-commercialism

The cold war is over. Capitalism triumphed over socialism. We have a time of peace and prosperity; of goods and services unimaginable to our parents and grandparents. Nearly everything (except housing) is getting cheaper.

And yet there are apparently more and more people who boycott, reject or simply rail against the consumer society. This is much more than the annual "Put Christ back into Christmas" campaign. This is the real thing: a new ideology.

The anti-commercialists hate advertising, marketing and sponsorship the most. If the medium is the message they certainly hate the media, but they are always happy to use it if they are ever offered the oxygen of publicity.

Their issues overlap, but here are the common complaints:

- Many firms *target children* to establish brand recognition. This causes them to manifest all manner of evils: pestering their parents, eating junk food, having false wants and then turning into nasty materialists.
- Firms constantly use *hidden advertising* and commercial trickery. This is the old "subliminal messages" nonsense, combined with a heady mix of being anti-infomercials, advertorials, product placement ... and the rest.
- *Offensive* advertising that sexes-up products and portrays sex as a commodity. It turns people, we are told, into either slaves or sex objects; causes and endorses harassment, even violence, against women.
- Worse, *advertising* lies and kills. It supports industries like the diet industry and the cosmetics industry that mislead with unsubstantiated promises. Further it encourages the taking of drugs that are known to be addictive, like alcohol, making their consumption look sexy.
- More *intrusive* marketing everywhere from junk mail to telemarketing. This is an attack on billboards and other forms of outdoor marketing, as well as video monitors in public places running ads in an interminable loop.
- Subtle *sponsorship* of sporting, cultural or civic groups by befriending and then bankrolling many kinds of organizations, such as schools,

hospitals, museums, but particularly sports groups, to wear logos everywhere.

- *Controlling television channel programming* through sponsorship of channels and indeed whole programs. This is particularly the case with home shopping and interactive television.
- The *commercialization of religious and civic holidays*: Christmas, Easter, public holidays. Turning social occasions into rites of consumption.
- *Encouraging waste* with over packaging, abuse of the earth, waste of fossil fuels. This is the current craze to find the blame for global warming.

So the rallying cry of the anti-commercialists? The consumer society, through its promotion of materialism, not only destroys civil and religious institutions, destroys the planet and ruins our health, but also steals our time and money and twists our minds.

If only marketing had that power, which is of course relative. Certainly, many adults appear to be "less savvy" than a lot of children. The favorite activities of the anti-commercialist are boycotts, demonstrations, letters of complaint. They complain that commercials spawn intrusive, manipulative, noisy and totally ubiquitous advertising, but often don't use it themselves to promote their position. Would that be hypocritical? If advertising is so powerful why not use it to their own advantage?

There is more than enough government legislation to "protect" consumers if indeed that is what they want. It's easy and naïve to blame all societal woes on commercialism.

And who has the hidden agenda in all this? Anti-commercialists target religious groups and make openly political and personal attacks on individuals lawfully engaged in business. If their attacks are ethically based they have this right – and the business equally has the right to respond. If on the other hand the attackers are falsely claiming that the business is operating illegally then the business can, and no doubt will, sue them.

Of course there are drawbacks of the consumer society. Of course there are abuses of advertising, and fashion victims and those who would rather have than be. But naïve Naderism is often more about apportioning blame for changes in society than any realistic analysis of human behavior.

The art and science of haggling

What is the difference between purchasing a carpet in the Grand Bazaar in Istanbul and buying a new car (with trade-in) in your local showroom? In one sense everything, but in another very little because both require astute, artful, assiduous bargaining skills. It pays to know how to haggle, perhaps more now than ever.

On a daily basis most of what we purchase carries a fixed advertised price. You can try (but will be rather misguided) to negotiate the price of stamps at the post office, baked beans at the grocery store or novels at airport bookstores.

But have you ever tried chatting up your local barperson, fruit and vegetable merchant or baker? Have you ever dared suggesting to a hotel desk clerk that you deserve a discount because it is so late in the day?

Most of us are (relatively) comfortable with the idea of the volume discount, the cash discount and the upgrade. *Bogof* (buy-one-get-one-free) is now very much part of our national psyche and our parents did "discount for cash." But all this is about negotiating around an advertised price. What if there are no guidelines?

Some car showrooms show the shiny new models without those loud numbers alluringly displayed on their roofs. "What would you like to pay for this car?" the young salesman has been encouraged to ask. And your skillful reply? It is not "nothing" or "a couple of hundred quid." Indeed it is best not to give an answer at all. For the question is a sales trick. "The best price for you and me" should stop that sort of nonsense.

There is a science – well, social science – and an art to the haggling process. The science is in *understanding* the process, the art in the *theatre* of the process.

As economists know, very specific factors affect the prices of products. There are robust laws of supply and demand. Prices are also affected by competition. Further macroeconomic and socio-political forces can very suddenly change the value of products.

The carpet seller in the bazaar; the salesman on the forecourt; the craftsperson at the fair all have fixed and variable costs. Unless they are in a genuine clearance sale or some equivalent, they usually have a very clear idea of the minimum price for which they are prepared to part with an object to earn a "reasonable living." This concept is, granted, rather slippery. Anything above the amount is good news.

Most sellers can tell stories of the amazingly naïve, careless, or loaded buyer who seems completely price-insensitive. They accept the preposterous "first asking price." So much so that many incredulous salespeople wished they had started even higher. So they have experience of great range. They know there is a bottom, but probably no top. And, like spiders, they wait and watch.

Their task is to size up the customer quickly. They call it "cold reading" in the astrology and tarot card reading business. Look at their age and stage. Get clues to their wealth and taste. Look at jewelry, shoes. Look at what they are carrying or, if you can, the car they arrived in. Where are they coming from? How much do they have? What is their mood state? How interested are they?

Then come the product display and explanation. Watch and listen for signs of interest and agreement. Pace it well. Mention the quality, not the price. List the benefits. Flatter their taste. Offer tea or coffee and, when and if they seem to have settled on something, start with a "best price" offer.

The rules of bargaining then ensue: Never accept the first offer; make the negotiator happy; ask "what if" questions, take your time; generosity is not contagious; shock them with a credible opening move, let your opposite start to haggle – negotiating is about trading not conceding; ask all those "How much off if . . ." questions, don't change the price, change the package, search for packages of potential solutions . . . and so on.

The art is in the performance. There are lots of features here that are important. Play the role of the expert, but accommodate to their style, language and so on. Adjust to their mode of speech, display your deep knowledge and love of the product.

It's a bit like speed dating. Ask the right questions. And be prepared for a few emotional displays when they are required: "hurt" when a low price is offered; "surprise" when they challenge your word.

Asking simple questions

There is a modern myth about the development of the toothpaste tube which is very illustrative. A curious – in both senses of the word – inventor approached a toothpaste manufacturer with a very simple idea. He persuaded the manufacturer to part with a six-figure sum on the promise his idea would quickly lead to seven-figure profits.

The idea? Double the width of the nozzle of the tube. People will then use at least twice as much each time they brush their teeth because the amount used is usually a function of the length of the brush. And as a follow-up suggestion? Persuade toothbrush manufacturers to produce bigger (that is longer) brushes.

An idea which costs so little can make so much. Studies of toothpaste tubes in the 1950s and 1960s have indeed demonstrated this to be true. In fact those little mini-tubes found in airline toilet bags prove how unsatisfactory they are.

It is an "invention" designed to increase consumption. Many products try this solution. Shampoos entreat you to "rinse *and repeat*" but few do. Suddenly ketchup manufacturers have given up the old glass bottle that required a mighty thump to move the first helping of sauce on to the plate. The bottles are now plastic to allow squeezing, they are stored up-side down to ensure a quick release of whatever is in the bottle and the sauce is "runnier" so that it flows out of the bottle faster. All round it's easier to use more product.

Some of the most useful office and home items are really simple and it seems difficult to imagine life without them: the paperclip (invented 1900); the ballpoint pen (1938); the pocket calculator (1971); the post-it note (1981). A few home inventions have transformed the lives of homemakers: the washing machine (1907); the food mixer (1919); the steam iron (1920) and the microwave oven (1947).

The lives of those doing the cooking have been forever transformed by the teabag (1919); sliced bread (1928); instant coffee (1937); aluminum foil (1947) and fish sticks (1955). Transportation has benefited (mostly) from traffic signals (1914); the parking meter (1935); cats' eyes, road studs (1935) and the car seat belt (1959).

The development of new products comes about by three simple processes. The first is to invent something new – something novel and useful that people want and need. Some products are flash-in-the-pan ideas like the hula hoop or the Popsicle but others can transform everything. Sometimes it's the development of a material like the aerosol (1926); polythene (1933); Teflon (1938) or Velcro (1956). Sometimes it is about finding a new packaging: the milk carton (1951); the ring top/pull top (1962) or cling wrap (1958).

Anything that makes life easier (the grocery store trolley, 1937), cheaper (the disposable syringe, 1955; disposable lighter, 1970), safer (suntan lotion, 1936; child-resistant cap 1971), more glamorous (bikini, 1946; hairspray, 1949; silicon implants, 1962) or simply more fun (TV talk show, 1948; Moog synthesizer, 1964) catches on.

But there are two other apparently simpler and less creative ways of being really innovative. One is to take a product and make it better: stronger, safer, more tasty. Compare domestic appliances like the kettle or the oven or the food mixer with those of 20, 40 or 60 years ago. They're made of different things, designed to be more reliable, more user-friendly and, equally important, more attractive.

The third way to be inventive is to question why things are done as they are and to stop doing things. Then do first-principle re-engineering. Perhaps the best example of this is the "cheap flight" entrepreneurs who have changed air travel for ever. Seats don't recline; they don't have pockets; they are not assigned. The problem of sluggish boarding is replaced with the very opposite. A massive scramble: survival of the fittest.

The third way is to ask others to justify why things are done, or not done, in a particular way. A popular question at the moment concerns the automation of jobs. Why employ a person when you know you could have a machine? Another involves the better use of time and space. Why not have 24-hour operations? Why not turn bars into cafés until opening times? Why not have mini-marts at every filling station? Why not have restaurants in bookstores?

Thinking through the use of people, time, space and technology can be most creative of all. Profit is the mother of invention. One of the most important things to do in any business is to step back and ask some simple but fundamental "why?" questions. Why make it, serve it, process it this way and not another? It can lead to radical changes.

Bad-mouthing products

One of the great problems of those ubiquitous hotel room feedback forms is that the delighted–dissatisfied rating scale rarely allows one to distinguish between levels of real displeasure. One can be not merely and rather coolly dissatisfied but seriously, hotly and furiously "pissed-off" – angry, fuming, vengeful, even apoplectically inarticulate with rage – about what did or did not occur.

Filling out the forms might help a little. It usually results in a poncy, crypto-grovelling, standard-format letter from the managing director some weeks later. No revenge there then. You could complain immediately by phone, or later at reception while queues of weary but impulsive businesspeople seek quick checkouts.

There are ways to "upgrade" the complaint. There are skills to be learnt in becoming a fully-fledged brand terrorist. Write, personally, to every member of the board or to the editor of the top trade magazine. Write to or phone industry analysts.

But the easiest response is consistent bad-mouthing of the place. Word-of-mouth communication is powerful. The marketing guys call it negative-valenced, informal communication between private parties about the quality of goods and services. It is the social sharing of emotions about an experience. But why do people do it? What are the real psychological functions and possible benefits of bad-mouthing?

Bad-mouthing is essentially an emotional act. And emotions drive motivation. After all they share the same Latin root: "to move". Emotions mobilize action. They also give it direction and force. So anger drives revenge; regret drives attempts to improve.

Three Dutch researchers (Wetzer *et al.* 2007) have recently studied the bad-mouthing effect. They argue there may be eight different goals of this behavior:

- Comfort – seeking moral support and understanding.
- Venting – simply blowing off steam.
- Advice – seeking help and clarification over the experiences.
- Bonding – strengthening social bonds between consumers.
- Entertaining – social amusement in conversation.
- Self-presentation – managing one's image or impression.

- Warning – helping the recipient not make similar mistakes.
- Revenge – attempting to harm others.

They asked people to whom and when they first communicated their negative experiences. The answer was usually a partner, family or close friend and quickly. Interestingly the experience felt much the same irrespective of who the recipient was or how long one waited. However they did clarify the three most common and prominent emotions associated with these experiences: anger, frustration, irritation, disappointment, regret, uncertainty – in that order.

Their next study tried to link what people did with the emotion they experienced. Pretty straightforward hypothesis – anger leads to revenge, regret to social bonding and so on. They found the eight goals could be described parsimoniously along two dimensions: focused at self vs. others; and constructive–destructive. Venting and revenge were most destructive and clearly linked to anger, frustration and irritation. Regret was related to bonding, entertaining and warning.

Perhaps one can read the goals of the bad-mouthers from the way they tell their story. Is it funny or questioning; bitter or moralistic?

But the real worry is the angry customers who don't vent in an orgy of bad-mouthing. These may be the strong, anger-in types who, like some criminals, plan their attack alone. Their focus is not on making themselves "feel better" but on punishing their service-providers. Their anger is cold, not hot; calculating not impulsive. It has more to do with sadistic punishment than restorative justice.

Some people never bad-mouth even after terrible service. Perhaps they are lacking in assertiveness. Possibly they believe it does no good. Some pursue the arsonist rather than trying quite simply to put out the fire. Some bad-mouth only *in extremis*. Others appear perpetually pissed off with a rich anthology of stories of bad service. And finally there are ambulance-chasing types eager to blow out of proportion the smallest incident for massive, disproportionate compensation.

Bad-mouthing is a coping strategy related to personality variables. And if personality predicts consumption preference it means some poor companies have more than their fair share of negative reviews.

Reference

Wetzer, I., Zeelenberg, M. and Pieters, F.G.M. (2007) " 'Never Eat in That Restaurant, I Did!' Exploring Why People Engage in Negative Word-of-Mouth Communication," *Psychology and Marketing*, 24, 661–80.

The banality of leadership

Understanding the mind of the killer is for many as fascinating as trying to understand the mind of the saints. What inspired Mother Theresa seems as important as understanding the factors that drove Hitler or Stalin or Pol Pot.

Social scientists of many persuasions all seek to explain and understand the complex, unique and often contradictory behavior of great leaders, particularly in business or politics. Whence their rise and fall? What made them commit acts of great compassion, or evil, or simple stupidity?

There are essentially *three* takes on these questions. That of personality theorists, that of social psychologists and those of sociologists.

The personality theorist searches for an explanation in the essential nature – the dispositional attributes – of the individual. They focus on the makeup of the person which they see as the primary causal agent for explaining the behavior they observe.

Those who take the individual difference or dispositional perspective search for factors inside the individual to explain their behavior. Those who take this perspective may be rather odd bedfellows. Thus the Freudians search for early childhood trauma, while the trait theorists look for indicators of unusual personality profiles and geneticists happily examine DNA markers. What they share is the belief also held by individuals, that it is the makeup of people that is the primary driver of behavior.

Thus there are lists of traits or competencies that business researchers have identified in great leaders. Some of these concepts seem rather vague, like "takes the helicopter view," or "has emotional intelligence," while others seem pretty straightforward and easily measured, such as intelligence or stability.

Those who take this perspective also tend to be pessimistic about change. What you see is what you get. It isn't easy to change people radically – you might teach them new skills or behavioral repertoires, but essentially their makeup is fixed.

Against them are the contextualizing social psychologists who believe it is situational factors that most influence behavior. Perhaps the most influential psychology study of the last century was about obedience to authority. It demonstrated very forcefully the banality of evil: that pleasant, ordinary, educated people were, in effect, willing to electrocute to death a perfect stranger because some "white-coated" experimenter told them to do so.

There are dozens of fascinating studies that show how situational factors can turn ordinary people into vicious, egocentric demons or empathic, self-sacrificing heroes. We know that people's willingness to help at accident scenes has more to do with the number of other people present than their own personal courage.

Ordinary social situations are governed by social rules and social norms which most of us obey. They constrain and shape our behavior. Yes, people seek out and indeed change particular situations and settings, but they have powerful effects. And social psychologists look to explain good and bad leadership in these terms.

This perspective has the advantage of being upbeat and positive. The fact that people don't change much means little to the situationist. Change the situation, change the behavior. You can therefore engineer good leadership relatively easily by shaping the situation in which it can thrive.

The third perspective is, at least in one sense, the grandest. It's the system or society: the object of study by sociologists. "I blame society," says Homer Simpson, somewhat ironically.

Certainly the state in which we live powerfully shapes behavior. "The system," as hippies used to call it, is certainly made up of complex cultural, economic, historical, political and religious forces. Not that long ago it was common to be openly racist. Victorians thought it preposterous that women should vote. Their parents found it easy to justify slavery.

The state, the system, society (whichever you prefer) has immensely powerful forces to compel all kinds of behavior. The law is perhaps the most obvious. Anyone who has lived under an oppressive regime knows immediately the power it can wield to dictate particular behaviors. The state legitimizes and illegitimizes styles of leadership. It selects, shapes, condones and condemns certain styles of leadership. There is real power in the system. Note how quickly changes in taxation change behavior.

So – the bottom line? There are individual, situational and systematic factors that shape leaders. Dysfunctional leaders, like highly functional leadership, are a product of all three. Ordinary and extra-ordinary people can and do perform ordinary and extra-ordinary things, depending on the specific and general context. In this sense, evil or goodness can seem banal. It is not difficult to explain why good people do bad things and vice versa because of the constraints under which they act.

However talented, motivated and ideal an individual is for a leadership role, the organization can easily destroy the leader's ability to do a good job. And the organization, too, is constrained by the state in which it is located.

Blame it on the boss

Perhaps it should be viewed as an excellent homage to market forces. As soon as those clever-clever books appeared about how to ask seriously brilliant questions at selection interviews, so there became available various books on smart answers to smart questions. No wonder the selection interview is such a smoke-and-mirrors affair.

And so to the business of failure at work. Whence the alienated, under-performing, second-rater at work? We have known for eighty years that where it can be reliably measured, the best performer produces 2.5 times the output of the worst performer. Some people are able, dedicated, effective and others, alas, are not.

It has been argued that the single most important thing a manager needs to be able to do is diagnose and confront poor performers. Through selection, challenges, support and feedback, it is the job of all managers to get the most out of their staff. Leaders have additional issues such as strategy. But all need to get the best out of good people.

To cater for the bewildered manager, therefore, many books are now available. One is called memorably *Jerks at Work* (Lloyd 1999) and promises how to "deal with people, problems and problem people." Another is *Managing Difficult People* (Pincus 2004) and it implores you not to let "negaholics" rule your workplace. In a pretty standard treatment ten proto-typic difficult types are outlined, such as "The Complainer or The Whiner" and "The No People Skills Person."

Another book, just published, is called *A Survival Guide to Managing Employees from Hell* (Scott 2007). The first chapter is called "Bad Attitude," the second "Incompetence" and the third "Personal Issues." The author offers seven options for dealing with "Idiots, Whiners, Slackers and Other Workplace Demons," starting with a conversation or formal review, to immediate termination, report to the authorities and retaliation precautions.

Interestingly, tucked away near the end of the book is a short section called "Bad Employee or Bad Boss?" And twenty possible issues are briefly considered, including being a micro-manager or a sexual harasser.

But the books have moved on from bad to mad. In his book *From Difficult to Disturbed*, Laurence Miller (2008) believes problem people essentially have personality disorders. So avoidant and dependent personality disordered workers are "shrinkers and clingers" while the ever dangerous narcissists and psychopaths are called "preeners and predators."

If the supposition of the book is that difficult people are bad, it is interesting that there are long sections on strategies and techniques for dealing with the problem. On the other hand, if the book is predicated on the dysfunctional, disturbed, mad model it is much more about describing the types than managing them. Screen, counsel or discipline them out seems the only real message.

So, from the bosses' perspective, it's a case of the sad, the bad, and the mad that one needs to deal with. They are the cause: always, totally, self-evidently.

But of course the employees now have a selection of (exclusively American) books that nicely and neatly place the blame with the boss. Boot-on-the-other-foot behavior. One short book by the bestselling author of *Nasty People* is called *Nasty Bosses: How to Stop Being Hurt by Them Without Stooping to Their Level* (Carter 2004). So now we have a neat typology of nasty bosses that include the carrot-dangler, the invalidator, the noper and the anal-izer. The author believes nasty bosses dwell in nasty organizations.

But in a much bigger, more serious-looking book, though similar in style, "nasty" is replaced with "toxic." So, *Coping with Toxic Managers, Subordinates ... and Other Difficult People* (Hibit 2004) takes a more clinical approach with narcissistic, grandiose and antisocial managers as well as those who are control freaks and unethically opportunistic, ruthless and bullying, even homicidal. And the book tells us how to use emotional intelligence to survive and prosper. The book belongs to the clinical school that sees toxicity as madness. Another book that proudly boasts it is based on surveys of more than 50,000 people is called *Thirty Reasons Employers Hate Their Managers* (Katcher 2007). It is the story of "why morale and productivity are low, turnover is high and loyalty non-existent." So there are 30 chapters under 5 headings.

The list is incredibly self-evident and dull. So "We're understaffed;" "We need more training;" "I'm not fairly paid." After 190 pages of what the other books would call negaholic whining we get less than 1½ pages of what you (the boss) can do. They are: listen to your employees, involve employees in developing solutions and start small and big things will happen.

And guess what the author of the book about employees from hell has (helpfully) written? *A Survival Guide for Working Bad Bosses* (Scott 2005).

The books are remarkably similar in appearance, size and print, possibly suggesting the "blame" may be equal.

And these managers from hell are called bullies, idiots and backstabbers. So there is the "Not Fit for Command" boss, the "Critically Clueless" and the "Dishonest Genius" while under the "Out of Bounds" section we have the "Intrusive Boss" and the "Party Planner."

At the end of the book you rate your boss on fifteen issues from sex in the office to decisiveness. And we get some "General Guidelines" about what to do if they are too rigid, or too emotional or too invasive. And here the solution is visualization (options, outcomes) rather than emotional intelligence.

One certainly gets a strong sense of a litigious culture when reading these books. It would be interesting to know about sales. Because there are more employees than bosses, possibly the Bad Boss books do better.

Certainly they all balance the "sad," "bad," "mad" trilogy one way or another. Those that stress "sad" offer most strategies for coping. Those that see underperformance as a moral, ethical issue of course resort to formal procedures and then the law. Without doubt the most interesting are the books that stress mental illness as the cause and see deselection, outplacement or any other euphemism as the best solution.

Few look at how these poor souls were selected in the first place or whether organizational culture, climate and procedures both cause and maintain incompetence or promote toxicity. The individual is erroneously seen as the sole cause of everything.

It's a funny world of us and them. And when you are unhappy at work it's always them. What you need is a quick, easy, cheap, fix-it solution. Hence the books. Demand meets supply.

References

Carter, J. (2004) *Nasty Bosses: How to Stop Being Hurt by Them Without Stooping to Their Level*. New York: McGraw-Hill.

Hibit, R. (2004) *Coping with Toxic Managers, Subordinates ... and Other Difficult People*. Upper Saddle River, NJ: Prentice-Hall.

Katcher, B. (2007) *Thirty Reasons Employees Hate Their Managers*. New York: Amacom.

Lloyd, K. (1999) *Jerks at Work: How to Deal with People Problems and Problem People*. Franklin Lakes, NJ: Career Press.

Miller, L. (2008) *From Difficult to Disturbed*. New York: Amacom.

Pincus, M. (2004) *Managing Difficult People*. Cincinnati, OH: Adams Media.

Scott, G. (2005) *A Survival Guide for Working Bad Bosses*. New York: Amacom.

Scott, G. (2007) *A Survival Guide to Managing Employees from Hell*. New York: Amacom.

Breaking the code

All skillful people have learnt graciously to accept hideous presents; to comment on appalling dress-sense with tact; to applaud a dire performance. Through irony, wit and inflection it is not difficult to both save face and also give feedback. But you need to know the code. So "We must get together for lunch sometime" is best understood by replacing sometime with never.

And how, politely, to disagree with someone on the offences of politics, religion or the opposite sex? Many choose from: "How interesting!", "If you say so" and "I don't disagree entirely."

Then there is the preface to feedback on incompetent work: "You have obviously worked hard on this," "I appreciate your contribution," "Help me understand how you saw the problem this way."

In the world of business the codes are usually simpler. So there is positive spin where "stress" becomes "challenge" and "a problem" is "an opportunity." "Leveraging resources" means "working all hours."

"I will never lie to you" means "The truth changes often." "I really appreciate your contribution" means "you have been wasting your time and effectively contributed nothing."

"Blamestorming" as it is now called means many people have to find ways of protecting themselves if their whole project goes badly wrong. So the strategy is to find some naïve person and say: "I really appreciate your being in on this one," or "We want you to champion the project," or "Help us syndicate the problem." "Please note and initial the document" means "We have it in writing that you agreed."

Temporary job titles may be coded: "individual contributors" means some poor sod who does all the work; "Manager special projects" is a sidelined, derailed senior manager pulled out of doing any more damage; "Coordinator Eastern Europe," likewise.

One can also take an approach from different departments. Thus, "to put on a marketing hat" means to lower ethical standards; "to bring in health and safety at this point" is to ensure the whole thing is scuppered; "to take a financial raincheck" means it will never be funded.

Other common phrases need careful translation. "You need to be more flexible" means "You have to do it my way." "You need to be more proactive" means "It's too late to get help now." "Your ideas are a trifle premature" means "They threaten me too much." "You appear to be suggesting a paradigm shift" means "That is stupid and wrong."

There are many polite ways to block anything. "That approach is on hold;" "You don't seem to appreciate there are bigger issues at stake;" "We have tried that and it didn't work."

Single phrases can be borrowed from marketing-speak. So "value-added" is expensive, "energy-saving" is under-powered; "low-maintenance" means simple, unfixable and disposable when broken. "All-new" means you can't get parts and is liable to breakdown; "rugged" means ugly, heavy and badly designed. "Additional features" means unnecessarily complicated and difficult to operate. "Breakthrough" means quirky, odd, not proven yet. "Testing phase" means constant failures. "Ethically sourced" means substandard and expensive.

Management- and marketing-speak are new tongues. Americans love new verbs. So you *anonymize* an idea and absorb the success of others by *assmosis*. You *bird-table* discussions in groups. You *bottom-fish* for cheap stocks and you *cybernate* ideas. To eat at your desk is to work *al desco,* while to tell stories of past success is to *anecgloat.* A *clocksucker* is an unproductive, incompetent worker and a *contrarian* someone who (productively) goes against the flow.

And never forget the power of the acronym. It's a CLM if you don't CYA because of your CPB. (It's a *career-limiting move* not to *cover your ass* if you get caught *conducting personal business*.) "He always talks BDNs but really he's a BHNC." (He talks *big damn numbers* but is all talk and no action: *big hat no cattle*.) The report is b.s. (not naughty: it stands for bloated syntax). A C-change is a change at the top often because the CEO has been a C-gull with the habit of flying off and leaving a huge mess for others to clean up. And then the annoying *advertorial*, and *coopetition*.

To have fun with language is one thing. To obfuscate or confuse is another. All secret societies have their own lingo. Indeed all groups seek to pass on messages that are unclear to other groups. We sugar the pill too – and it leads to mysterious codes. Lexical cryptography, not perfidious Albion.

Business virtues

Many cultures believe that giving a child a particular name will somehow (magically) allow them to inherit that particular quality. Thus Victorians called a child Faith, Charity or Constance. Africans do the same. At home we once had Beauty the cook and Knowledge the gardener.

But names are highly prone to fashion. As are virtues. Certainly there are the classic virtues. In his Social Affairs Unit book provocatively entitled *Decadence*, editor Digby Anderson (2005) contrasts some old with new virtues.

In the past, the authors argue, people were brought up to believe in different things from today. Virtues inform values which inform behavior. This is partly why some organizations have discovered the older worker. They are a cohort brought up in a different world. They have values of the past that are so important today.

What are the old virtues? First, *prudence*: self-control and self-moderation. Perhaps it is the opposite that we see in our youth today. Then there is *courage*. Some organizations have brought this back as a competence. There are, of course, many types of courage: risk-taking, interpersonal, moral and physical. It is about resolve, tenacity, fortitude: the virtues of leaders like Shackleton are now being discovered.

And then there is *love*. Love of one another: the heart of charitableness. And what of *thrift*? Such an oldfashioned word. It is about not wasting resources, taking the concept of stewardship seriously.

A forgotten virtue is *disinterest*: neutrality, impartiality, integrity. It means not taking sides. It means following the code. It is the greatest of all administrative virtues. And finally the family virtues of *obedience, authority, understanding one's role in the hierarchy.*

Would you value a prudent and thrifty, courageous and fair, kind and logical worker? Of course, who wouldn't? But can you find them? Indeed, but they may be in short supply because we have new virtues. Virtues for the twenty-first century. Virtues subtly different from the old virtues. Sounding much the same; chiming with the zeitgeist but different, very different.

These days we do justice: social justice and distributive justice. It used to mean assigning rewards and responsibilities to people based on merit. But merit or desert has been replaced by fairness. So charity, philanthropy, magnanimity are replaced by distribution rules or mechanisms. The idea is now to reduce all inequalities. No bad thing of course, unless it encourages bureaucracy, tyranny, or even worse, a different type of inequality.

We now do green virtues and caring virtues and therapy virtues. Green virtues can grow into vices because so many trade-offs have to be made. Caring is good, as long as people can and will take responsibility. "Care in the community," argued some, was a simple slogan to justify closing down hospitals and throwing people out onto the streets.

And now help-seeking is a virtue. Self-help, stoicism and self-sufficiency are scoffed at. You need, you must have, you will benefit, from – a therapist. You need self-understanding: discovering your inner something or other.

The greatest of the new business virtues? Accountability and transparency. Ah – but accountable to whom? All the stakeholders. Indeed, but what if they, and they surely do, have very different, powerfully conflicting needs and wants? People are faced with incompatible, inconsistent objectives and told to legally and transparently solve them.

Further transparency can and does lead to subtle secrecy. The more people are able to access material, the less is actually written or is written in code. Try doctors' notes. Consider appraisal forms.

And the final straw: a spirit of consistent criticism. This is not the virtue of curiosity, not the spirit of intellectual questioning. Rather it is the spirit of challenge, of suspicion, almost of paranoia. Every authority, every law, every order warrants challenge.

The sharing and caring, green and accountable, critical and self-insightful boss and company. Indeed. But virtues, old and new, can become vices, particularly to the degree and extent to which they are enforced.

Reference

Anderson, D. (ed.) (2005) *Decadence*. London: Social Affairs Unit.

The business convergence hypothesis

Many people lament the fact that all high streets seem alike. Even the new malls give one dramatic *déjà vu*. Same shops, same products, same prices.

For some, this represents a wicked takeover by greedy, process-obsessed chains, some foreign-owned, many multinational. They say, contrary to the evidence, that they have less choice and higher prices. Often the reverse is true, particularly with prices.

It's a matter of very simple economics that the small trader cannot compete and their prices are higher. And astute competitors soon notice if a chainstore is enjoying the profits of near monopoly. They come in to challenge them. Competition means lower prices.

But worse than high streets all looking the same, foreign towns look the same too. Walk through a shopping street in Paris or Prague, Melbourne or Marbella, Atlanta or Athens and there they are: the same big stores with the same products. Prices may be somewhat different but it's the same products and the same brands.

Call it dull, homogenous globalization, or sensible business convergence. The same is happening in the service industry, be it restaurants or air travel. The staff may be local, but that is all: the process is universal.

Apart from the spread of multinationals some see young people as "losing their culture", taking up a sort of mid-Atlantic outlook. Through better education via the web, foreign travel and student exchanges young people are becoming similarly Westernized, modern citizens of the world. They see things in the same way and work in the same way.

This is not the end of history, it's the end of culture argument. Well at least corporate culture. But is that true?

Take the concept of good service. Think of international airlines. The reason why we have air miles is that by and large we can't tell the difference between one airbus or jumbo and the next. We take safety and cleanliness for granted. So apart from price and timetable, it's only the service that differentiates airlines. And they know it, and struggle with it.

Are there really fundamental differences in the concept of good service? Do hotels in Vietnam differ from those in Venezuela in what they try to provide? Certainly local "mom and pop" hotels should be strong indicators of local ways in what is or is not provided. It can be charming to enjoy the "rustic simplicity" of the room above the taverna on the Greek island. Cold showers, salad for breakfast and pretty rough wine all seem part of the experience.

But we all want clean and quiet and have come to expect certain things. We want service people to be well-informed, polite and attentive. We expect them to be cleanly and neatly turned out. Perhaps there are cultural differences in the extent to which we want our waiters to be "respectful" or "friendly." The American way of introducing oneself and sharing a potted life-history is unlikely to go down well in Japan, but the fundamentals are the same.

To any Third- or Second-Worlder, a Marks & Spencer, Tesco or Wall-mart is paradise, assuming they have First-World wages to spend. There is choice, reliability of supply and competitive pricing. Perhaps it's only those sentimental baby boomers who, when on vacation, like the high street of some quaint town to stay caught in time. They don't seem to mind the lack of choice, the high prices, the unavailability of certain products.

Pubs, post offices and local shops close because they can't compete. Given the choice people vote with their feet and cars and trolleys. Some fight rearguard actions through local council planning to "preserve their identity" and other euphemisms for avoiding developments.

Funny how the same people deplore discrimination of all sorts, unless of course it is discrimination in where they choose to shop.

Convergence is unstoppable. See it as bland homogenization or a celebration of unity, it will continue to occur. Young people from all over the world share more than ever before. They see the world through similar eyes and want similar things.

In this sense there will be less need to "embrace diversity" because values, places of work and consumption will become ever more similar.

Business recovery

There are considerable data to support the perhaps counter-intuitive idea that if a particular "service delivery" fails in some way, but is recovered, people are more happy with the company than if the "cock-up" never occurred. No, this is not the world of compensation lawyers and court cases. It may not even involve money at all. A small spillage compensated by a free dessert, a late pizza delivery and you get it for free.

Business recovery is serious issue. The subject of *Harvard Business Review* articles, the argument is that investment in business recovery is really important. You can turn a dissatisfied customer into an evangelical proselyte for your organization, or the precise opposite: a marketing terrorist.

So a case-study. A frequent flyer bought a business class long-haul ticket costing over £3000. He needed to sleep flat, chose his seat both ways. He was not a systematic complainer, having only once in 25 years made a documented complaint. On this trip the seat did not recline on the way there, nor on the way back. And yes the flight was full – blah, blah, blah. And, his bags had been opened and things stolen.

Not good enough. Armed with a code number given at the airport to report stolen/opened luggage he filed an email complaint.

Recall our traveler is a frequent flyer: around 20 to 30 flights per year. All classes. Many destinations. He holds allegiance cards from four consortia and what dictates airline choice is timetable more than anything else. He does not always book his own tickets, but often nominates his preferred carrier. There was no fast reply. He went abroad for three days on four European flights – all tickets having been bought some time ago.

The day he was to book the next long-haul flight to the same destination he got a curt dismissive rebuff from the airline. It never mentioned the seat problem and said that the airline advises people to keep things of special value in their hand luggage.

So he chose another carrier. Things were much better, so he repeated the exercise a month later. Over the next six months where possible he chose not to fly with the problem carrier. Around £10,000 in ticket sales went to rivals.

Let's do the math. Imagine he was offered a free upgrade on his next flight; three lounge entries; even a slightly more subtle letter. The cost to the airline: maximum a couple of hundred pounds. The benefit the £10,000. Not rocket science: a no-brainer.

That is why hotel staff in some upmarket chains are given £100 in cash or more to help with business recovery. They have neither to spend it, nor even to account for it in detail. They *do* have to use their discretion as to why, when and on whom the money is spent.

So why don't organizations take business recovery more seriously? Some do. But it can be expensive. You need trained staff to answer phones and emails. It's not a great job and they need patience and skill and are poorly paid.

One reason senior managers pull the plug on the whole exercise or at any rate gradually starve it of resources, is the image of the greedy, dissimulating, professional complainer out to exploit the system for freebies. These types are well known as they attempt to cause maximum fuss or embarrassment to achieve compensation, completely out of proportion to any discomfort, inconvenience or even injury.

They do exist. They are pests. But the question is the proportion of the dishonest to honest complainers. If the former outnumber the latter there may be a good case to reject the business recovery ideas.

One low-cost airline has a CEO who appears to rejoice in being rude to customers. Perhaps the tactic is to attempt to prevent anyone from ever complaining. And yet the airline is massively successful. So, good evidence of the non-necessity of investing in business recovery, people, systems and compensation deals? Probably not. Big airlines know it is their business class frequent flyers who really bring in the revenue. Most have plenty of choice. And, better still, they choose but don't often pay for their tickets. They need to be nurtured. They are busy, tired and stretched but also high spenders.

The trick is trying to differentiate between the professional complainer and the genuine recipient of bad service. Gold card holders have their complaints taken more seriously of course. And so be it.

But the result of the case-study is that this traveler has turned into a brand terrorist. Previously a person to sing the glories of the airline, he now blasts their service. Fickle perhaps? And worse, he writes newspaper columns telling hundreds and thousands the story. Such robust retaliation suggests that the treatment of his complaint might itself have been a response to an existing antagonism. A large cost for a perfunctory brush-off.

The capture-bonded employee

Why do people continue to work for bullying, mean, abusive bosses? Because they have few alternatives? Because they don't see their boss like that? Because the boss has some strange hold over them?

Over 30 years ago a Swedish psychiatrist coined the term "The Stockholm Syndrome" to describe a puzzling case where bank employees taken hostage by bank-robbers for six days became emotionally attached to their victimizers. Some defended their captors after their ordeal was over. One woman broke off an engagement and remained loyal to a former captor while in prison. She remained bonded or in bondage: still a captive.

In fact the Stockholm syndrome is now more widely known as capture bonding. There have been numerous cases over the years, from the famous Patty Hearst story to the more recent case of the Austrian girl held captive for many years only to grieve her captor's suicide.

Most, but not all, cases involve sexual abuse and various forms of humiliation. The idea has seeped into popular culture and many fictionalized accounts of the manifestation of the syndrome. Movies, soap operas, novels echo the theme.

The mystery is how and why captives bond with their captors. Why they appear to fall in love with them and don't try to escape.

There are two not very similar "explanations" for this paradox. The psychoanalysts see it in terms of the *defense mechanism* of *identification*. Babies form emotional attachments to the nearest powerful adult to ensure survival. The hope is that this is a loving parent or parental figure.

Children have healthy bonding dispositions: needs for attachment. People bond in every situation: normal or abnormal. Early experiences shape later ones. Thus if people have felt captive by parents, friends, "carers" in their youth they will have a greater affinity to the "captive" lifestyle and be more easily capture-bonded.

Evolutionary psychologists peering into our ancestral past have a related idea. Being violently captured by another tribe was not that uncommon. So *social reorientation* when captured from one hostile group to another was an essential survival mechanism. Thus we all have wired-in knowledge of how to induce bonding in captives. We can all do it ourselves.

The syndrome is also evident in animals. The alpha male lion or gorilla takes over the group (pride, troupe). He first kills all the babies, causing the females to stop lactating and get back into season. He then mates with the females to produce his own genetic offspring.

So rather than being inexplicable, counter-intuitive and abnormal, it is an adaptive response hardwired for survival.

But does this explain, even in part, why people not only don't flee from but even protect toxic managers, bastards, bullies and bozos? In basic military training people are assaulted, humiliated and abused yet they come to respect then like the perpetrators. Is the same true in business?

If the theories are right, perhaps there need to be three things in place. If the Freudians are right there are those more or less prone to the capture bonding syndrome. As a result of childhood experiences they seem more vulnerable and probably in adulthood have a history of staying in abusive relationships, so feeling captive is normal. Indeed the captive-prone may be attracted to organizations where the work experience feels a bit like being captured.

Next, the abusive boss needs to be dominant, strong, unrivalled. He, and it almost always is he, is the attachment figure, the alpha male, the all-seeing Almighty all at the same time. Dare one point out that 90 per cent of Stockholm syndrome capture bonding cases show the victim to be female? This follows from evolutionary theory more than psychoanalysis, but makes sense. It also indicates those more likely to be victims.

Third, the work relationship is intense, certainly emotionally, possibly physically. It is about brute force, the bending of wills, being reprogrammed. Some bosses have these opportunities.

But is it just too fanciful, too psychobabbly ridiculous ever to imagine there could be such a thing as a (mildly) capture-bonded employee? A person who remains loyal, even peculiarly fond of an abusive, demanding, toxic boss? A person who does not try to find alternative employment when it is reasonably readily available? A person who defends her plainly guilty boss against many just accusations of immoral, illegal and unethical behavior? Never heard of this?

Perhaps the term captive-bonded employee is too loaded. Perhaps the explanation for the Stockholm syndrome is too unscientific. But nearly everyone can point to – at least in others – evidence of this puzzling and worrying behavior pattern.

Carrot and stick management

In the cartoons at any rate, there are (only) two mechanisms to get the donkey to move forward: carrot or stick. Promise of reward, threat of punishment. Prescriptive versus proscriptive corporate culture.

Ask people if theirs is a carrot or a stick culture and they immediately understand the question and therefore tend to give a quick, unequivocal answer. Which works best? Which is more efficient and effective for business growth, happiness, sustainability? The usual answer, mostly correct, is carrot works better than stick. But there are provisos.

Carrot management works best for extraverts in sales and marketing jobs. It probably works better for young people, for optimists and for those in the service industries.

Carrot management tends to be prescriptive. People receive clear guidance about what attitudes, behaviors and outcomes are desirable and are constantly rewarded for them. Carrot leaders believe in modeling what they want and are bent on shaping their staff by constant encouragement when things are done in the way they want.

Stick management aims to prohibit activities and behaviors that do not fit the model they are after. Managers aim to use mistakes as exemplars and rely on negative feedback to inhibit that which they don't want. Stick managers often say their style works because it is easy to understand, quick to do, and "the only thing the staff really understand and accept".

Of course, in practice, nearly all managers use both. But there does seem to be a naturally preferred approach. Like handedness, in that most of us lean to the use of the one hand or the other. But is it a case of dexterous carrot and sinister stick?

Some have argued that it is possible to differentiate carrot and stick leadership styles which reflect the personal, interpersonal and organizational approach and culture. But that does have a "four-legs-good–two-legs-bad" feel about it.

So the stick guys get all the bad words. They are defensive and constraining and negative. The good guys, our carrot tops, are praised for being constructive, facilitative and positive. Stick management is top-down, unilateral, unforgiving while carrot management is more open, more reciprocal, more hopeful.

Managers have lots to do. Whether or not they spend time and effort in vision, mission and values stuff, they do have to be clear in what they want from individuals, groups and departments. People need a sense of direction, of how things should operate and ideally someone providing an excellent role-model. So carrot managers define, model and reward that which they want.

Stickies tend to be more into damage limitation. They assume people (any fool) know what is required and the manager's job is to prevent them doing what they don't want or not doing what they do want. There is, in their view, a "correct way" to do everything and you will be punished until you do it that way. Amen.

Carrot managers love role-models and make examples of those who embody the spirit of the enterprise. Even the communists knew this and the word Stakhanovite entered the language as a prototype of heroic Stalinist work zeal. We might call it workaholic, work–life imbalance, obsession-ality. But that is what the directors of the Soviet economy wanted, so they found a hero and blessed him.

While carrots exemplify, sticks circumscribe. They dismiss, reject, refuse any ideas for doing things differently. They can be doctrinaire, but always know about how things should, can, may, not be done.

Carrot leaders believe in help. They go for coaches, mentors, tutors because they like the idea of good workers passing on their skills, attitudes and behaviors. So the best are chosen (and rewarded) for mentoring jobs. It becomes a badge of honor. They induct, grow, nurture staff – concentrating always, of course, on reward.

Stick managers tend to be a tad Darwinian. They let people learn from personal experience: sink or swim. Survival of the fittest. They are not so enthusiastic about all that expensive mentoring palaver. They believe smart people learn from their mistakes, quickly and cheaply.

And what of creativity, challenging assumptions, lateral thinking? If you are a sticky, forget it. Your job is rule-following. Your elders and betters are chosen for that task. Challenging approaches is more like insubordina-tion and disloyalty than being innovative. Carrot leaders, being optimists, tend to be happy with those offering new ideas.

Organizations have their stories, their myths and their cast. For the carrot leader the play is of swashbuckling heroes who exemplify the spirit of the quest. More Edmund Hillary than Captain Oates. A rejoicing in their victories, their strengths, their dedication and use of talents.

Stick management seems to wallow in stories of those who "crashed and burned," who did not "fit in" and who, because they did not follow the rules, failed to succeed. Remember the demise of "old so-and-so"; recall the fate of misfits, challengers and the rest.

Both carrot and stick managers can be, indeed should be, astute monitors of the performance of their staff. Carrot managers take interest in people. They look out for examples of excellent and exceptional performance. They focus on the how as much as the what is done and try to understand the process better. And they tend, by definition, to be liberal with praise and easy with real compliments.

Stick managers are certainly close monitors; some would call it micro management. They are supersensitive to differences, deviations and diversions from the norm. Their feedback, verbal and nonverbal, is quick, clear and critical. You only get called to the boss's office when you have done something wrong.

Most of us can remember carrot and stick schoolteachers. Both might have helped us secure better grades. But who is it that we remember with grateful thanks? Carrot teachers inspire by finding out what we are good at.

Over fifty years ago McGregor proposed the difference between managers who held theory X and those who held theory Y. The former are optimists who turn to carrot management because they believe in the dignifying concept of inherently intrinsically motivated workers who, if encouraged, will always give of their best.

Against them are the clear Hobbesians who believe workers are just another form of animal: selfish, lazy and feckless, who need strict guidance.

But stick managers have clearly never been to a dog show, a circus or a sea-life park and watched trainers in action. There are no sticks, but an abundance of species-appropriate carrots. No sticks not even *in extremis*. A dearth of carrots works better than a multitude of sticks.

The chain of happiness

Despite its commonsense appeal and its "obviousness", the service–profit chain theory is under threat. The revisionists from that most threatening school of thought – the evidence based brigade – have suggested that the evidence does not stack up.

The idea, first published in a *Harvard Business Review* paper and later in a successful book, was based on a causal chain model which led from employee satisfaction to profit. You read the boxes, encouraged by the model (little more than a pretentious word for a semi-random array of boxes and arrows) that suggest one (damn) thing leads to another.

On one extreme was the ultimate goal: profit. This was a function of repeat business from happy customers. It was the excellent ("delight, don't just satisfy me") service that did the trick. And this in turn was driven by good managers, a healthy adaptive culture and good management practice. Good managers choose and motivate good staff, who consistently deliver the golden goose. They do emotional labor and that pays off.

So – and this is the disputed bit – happy staff make happy customers. Certainly the obverse is patently true: alienated, disgruntled, demotivated service staff leak their feelings. The hapless customer is a despised and demanding nuisance. The service is poor, the customer never returns. Worse, they get angry, never leave tips, and complain. So the negative cycle accelerates.

There are two errors in the way the service–profit chain argument and model was interpreted. The first was that happy staff cause, bring about, or directly influence the happiness of their customers. It is a sort of satisfaction spillover model. The second is that it is their managers who are the most direct influences on that happiness. That is, management style brings about customer happiness.

There is no doubt that it is more fun to be served by someone who is happy. A natural smile is better than a forced one. A positive "can do" energy is far better than negative "nyet." But service is a skill and happiness a disposition. You need both for exemplary service.

At the heart of the error is perhaps the most common assumption in the whole world of management. That anything (everything) can be changed, trained, enhanced. It's part of that Disneyesque world of charming naïveté; of charlatans in Guruland; the bread and butter of the training industry.

Recently there have even been calls from distinguished economists to teach happiness in schools. The already overstretched curriculum will have to find space for lessons in happiness.

The data alas do not always fit the naïve view. Happiness is largely trait-like. It is stable over time and consistent across situations. Happy children grow into happy adults and vice versa. The stable extravert – the sanguine type – is consistently happy. Equally, neurotic introverts, those with negative affectivity who move away from people, are the most unhappy. You can't cure neurosis, but you can teach effective coping skills. And you can teach introverts to look like extraverts and they then become what is technically called socialized extraverts.

The data for the predispositional, unchangeable nature of happiness is impressive. One study looked at people who had major traumatic accidents and became quadriplegic. The other looked at those who won the lottery. Nightmare and dream. What the study revealed was that although both events had an enormous short-term impact on their wellbeing, within two years those affected had returned to the level of happiness they had before the event. Those most happy before regained that level of happiness and vice versa.

Managers can and do seriously upset their staff. They certainly have the power to demotivate even the most robust workers. People leave managers not organizations. And of course, the frail flowers, the negatively oriented merchants of gloom are easily distracted, disenchanted and dispirited. But equally the happy easily regain their equilibrium.

There is a weak relationship between happy staff and happy customers. It is always nicer dealing with those with inherently sunny dispositions. But their happy demeanor does not "come from" nor is "caused by" good management and appreciative customers. Staff at the customer interface will always need service skills training and appropriate management. But these do not in themselves create a service disposition.

In this sense there is no chain. No causal link. It means selection is as important as management – perhaps even more so.

Conscientizing the public

"We are not intimidating people," said the angry, ugly picket. "We are just attempting to conscientize them." It seems that the American belief in the inalienable right of every noun to become a verb is ubiquitous.

Where once we disembarked, we now deplane. You can auto condiment your food. We motivate for new products and Hoover the carpet.

The politically active, particularly those from various pressure groups, have found a new ugly neologism. They are attempting to "conscientize" people. Apparently the phrase originated in the liberation theology movement of the 1970s which felt it was the primary goal of the Christian message to help people understand the difference between right and wrong and act accordingly.

It is not clear whether the conscientizing brigade are trying to create a conscience, awaken a dormant and sleepy conscience or somehow change and massage an existing conscience.

A conscience is a moral sense or an inner feeling of right and wrong, goodness and badness. So the *conscience-stricken* are guilt-stricken, while *prisoners of conscience* are usually detained for expressing deeply held ideological views unacceptable to the state.

Colloquially one may declare "*in all conscience*", meaning by all that is fair. And then there is *conscience money,* a sum paid to relieve the conscience. You can have things *on your conscience*, troubling you and you can do things for *conscience's sake.*

To have a well-developed conscience, to be conscientious and to perform all tasks conscientiously are clearly good things. And to be conscienceless is certainly a moral problem. Psychopaths are also known by their old title of "moral imbeciles." They are characterized by many factors, the most fundamental of which is their lack of conscience.

So how does the conscience develop? Ah – the speculation of psychologists, educators and theologians. Certainly as yet there have been no attempts to find the conscience gene, though we do know there is evidence for the heritability of conscientiousness as a personality trait.

While the concept of original sin appears to have fallen out of favor there are these who believe in the innate depravity of all mankind (resulting from the consequences of the Fall). We have it seems simply the veneer of conscientiousness of morality, of empathy. A mask for selfishness, sinfulness and seediness.

But most are with the Freudians, who at least see the conscience as starting out as neutral. We are said by old Sigmund to be *polymorphous perverts* – that is our wickedness can take many forms. We are putty in the hands of our parents who are the primary conscience-educators. For the Freudians the conscience is the superego and the theory of its development is that it is concerned with ideals. It has two parts: ego ideal and conscience. The former sets standards of behavior; the latter is concerned primarily with preventing morally objectionable behavior and thoughts.

These develop gradually during childhood as children learn to control unacceptable behavior because they come to understand it is likely to be met with both passive disapproval but also active punishment. Children are not naturally good. So a combination of fear of consequences and conscience are the primary mechanisms of self-control.

This account therefore sees early parental socialization and cultural issues as being major factors in the development of a conscience. The question is whether there is a critical period for the development of a conscience or whether it can be trained later in life.

Do consciences become dimmed? Do they rust? Are they twisted by evil forces and evil people? Did the German people who gave us Goethe and Faust and innumerable composers lose their conscience under the Third Reich? Did evil become so banal and commonplace that the conscience was "switched off"? And if so what should be done to switch it back on? Remove state terror? Hold free and fair elections? Reinstate the rule of law?

In a famous book from over 30 years ago the arch-behaviorist Skinner spoke of "Beyond Freedom and Dignity." He might well have mentioned conscience. The behaviorists are not interested in any of those metaphysical concepts like soul, conscience or superego, which they see as quaint superstitions that neither explain nor predict human behavior.

If, and when, we act with conscience we are doing it for a rich mixture of reward and punishment. Conscience is a way of describing a behavior pattern that we know to be good for the group. People are not good because they have developed a fine sense of justice, morality or whatever. They behave that way because they have been consistently and clearly rewarded for it and indeed punished for not behaving appropriately. So yes, you can conscientize people – but this is not a one-off event. People, like animals, need extensive training and an environment that offers consistent reinforcement.

Common rooms, canteens and cubicles

What is the best predictor of staff morale? Pay and conditions? Job security? Personal autonomy and control? Corporate culture? Managerial skills? Does it all depend on factors such as the personalities of the workers? The state of the economy? One individual manager? Or are there universals that apply?

Big organizations with multiple similar sites, such as grocery stores, bars and filling stations, can and do ask the question and try to provide the answer. One chain of public houses tried to establish which factor best predicted revenue and profit. The pundits speculated that it was location or parking lot, or hot food, or the number of "guest beers". It turned out to be the toilets – how clean, spacious, and abundant they were. The toilets not only encouraged women, and thence families, but were a good index of the type of manager they had. Clean toilets lead to happy and returning customers. And as pubs, clubs and restaurants know, the value of customer loyalty is crucial.

A well-known grocery store chain did likewise. Their results did not surprise them. It was the size, comfort and food available in the canteen. It's pretty relentless, stacking and packing, or sitting at a checkout. The common room, canteen or whatever the back room is called is "off stage." It provides respite. You can kick off your shoes, shoot the breeze, read the paper. You have choice. You can have a good moan or practice your counseling skills. You can have something to eat, even sleep.

The size and facilities in the common room are crucial because of the different options they offer. A cramped, overused kitchen with a kettle, microwave and toaster seem to offer a hot-bunking opportunity to refuel. They can easily get very grubby. They can also become a bit whiffy, especially if people microwave strong-smelling food.

The trouble is, of course, square footage. We work in open-plan offices not to encourage interaction or facilitate communication, but to save on space. We labor in cat-swinging, Dilbert-like cubicles because the organization deems it more space-efficient.

Some have wisely turned the public areas into atriums of light with tropical plants, e.g. British Airways in its famous Waterside corporate headquarters, as do many City firms. But it is a big investment of architectural planning, and, quite simply, space.

So the "relaxation" facilities are really important. But then so are the working facilities. This is an issue not only of the ergonomics of your office chair, the power of your computer or the filing system. It is about proximity and propinquity.

Your friendship groups at work are less about your values, demographics, personality or preferences and more to do with your daily contact. You tend to get friendly with those you see most often. Those you bump into. That is why the people nearest the photocopier, the watercooler and the locked door become well known. Smokers huddling together outside the building form social groups.

One executive at a failing institution recently insisted that everybody – yes, everybody – move office. His aim was to break up cabals, to destabilize the organization. To unfreeze before refreezing. Anyone who has experienced an office move knows this well. New relationships are formed, others wither over time.

Those you see most often you get to know – and frequently like. Organizational silos occur for many reasons, but they are maintained primarily through propinquity. Put all the finance people together on one floor, in one building and they soon develop silo thinking. Distribute them physically throughout the organization and you break this down.

We are social animals. The quality and quantity of social contact within the workplace should not be underestimated. It is one of the drivers of job satisfaction. And it can be, in part, environmentally engineered.

Don't underestimate the significance of building layout. Money spent on improving the "back areas" such as the canteen and the common room may generate disproportionate returns. And you can powerfully influence informal networks, teams and "us–them" thinking simply by rearranging where people work.

Consumer boycotts

There are many ways consumers can "flex their muscles." A very old strategy is the boycott, which is in essence an attempt to achieve a particular objective by urging individual consumers to refrain from selected purchases in the marketplace.

The Americans in the 1760s and the Indians in the 1930s both used boycotts as a political weapon against their colonial masters, namely us. Today we have brand boycotts, commodity boycotts, single firm-boycotts. Some are media-based, others marketplace-focused.

There are some interesting distinctions to be made with respect to boycotts. First there is the *time* issue. They can be long-, medium- or short-term affairs. Next there is *place* – that is how geographically distinct it is. Third, completeness – total or partial. Next there is the boycott *sponsor*: religious, political, environmental, ethnic groups. Fifth there are the actions taken: you can request a boycott, or organize a boycott in the street, or in the media. There are regular "blacklist" boycotts, which specify what not to buy, as well as positive "whitelist" boycotts, which specify what you should buy.

And there are *obstructionist* boycotts which can place obstacles in the way of those trying to buy the boycotted product or service. There are *expressive* boycotts, more about venting frustration than anything else.

We have to consider different *targets* of boycotts. So we have travel boycotts about going to a particular area; headquarters boycotts and so on.

Boycotts have been studied by political scientists who have come to a specific conclusion regarding what factors affect their success. Friedman, in his comprehensive book on the topic (Friedman 1999), suggests ten factors that help ensure that media-oriented, image-tarnishing boycotts work.

- Have a well-known person or group announce the boycott.
- The announcement should clearly target particular products, services or organizations.
- The boycott rationale should be simple, straightforward and appear legitimate.
- The start of the boycott should be as dramatic as possible.
- Attempts should be made to make the media coverage of the boycott as widespread and top-of-mind as possible.

- The more image-conscious the target of the boycott the more vulnerable they are.
- If the target thinks that all the media hype will lead to marketplace, behavioral boycott.
- The more negative, inflexible, complacent or non-adaptive the target of the boycott is in their reaction, the more realistic the boycotters' demands appear to be.
- The less capable the boycott target is at launching a successful counter-action against the boycotters.

Those who aim less at the media than the marketplace itself know they must be focused. The target of the boycott should be clear. The boycott should be well-timed – that is there should be no competing boycotts. Third, the public can easily and reasonably find a substitute for the boycott services. The effect of any boycotted activities should be highly visible.

The history of boycotts is very interesting. There have been labor, minority-group and religious-group boycotts. But these days boycotts seem mainly to be consumer and ecological. The latter are multiplying with the new carbon obsession. Famous examples in the past have concerned tropical timber, particular fish (tuna), or animal testing but now the principal targets are over-packaging and fuel wastage.

Remember the anti-apartheid boycott against firms engaged in trade and investment in South Africa? Or boycotts again GAP and NIKE because of the alleged misuse of child labor? Did they work or did they backfire?

Boycotts are of course about ideology. This is reflected in the demo-graphics of those who support and indeed lead many boycotts, especially consumer and ecological boycotts. They tend to be young, middle-class, politically left, well educated. Interestingly the data suggest that women get more involved than men, perhaps because they do more of the shopping.

The art and science of boycotting seems to be advancing. It is no longer an activity for angry amateurs. The boycotters are now students of mar-keting. They are becoming sophisticated in their slogans. They orchestrate national, even international days of protest. They involve (as cute as pos-sible) children as activists. They advertise: they certainly have become media-savvy. Many appear to condone (minor but illegal) disobedience in their cause.

Some even employ marketing experts to help them. Thus an agency may be in the unusual position of having two competing clients: the one trying to push a product or service; the other trying to destroy it.

To the skeptic they are little more than politically motivated hypocrites. They are fundamentalist utilitarians who believe that anything they do justifies the end. So they act just like those they accuse. Successful boycotts can have very serious and unplanned repercussions. Firms fail; people are paid off; customers just switch brand.

So are boycotts ultimately a conscience-oriented, effective weapon of the weak, or a crypto-political and cynical manipulation of the naïve?

Reference

Friedman, M. (1999) *Consumer Boycotts.* New York: Taylor & Francis.

Corporate courage

Fortune favors the brave, particularly in business. Or does it? Certainly cowardice, pusillanimity and weakness in the face of adversity are bedfellows of failure.

Courageous leaders inspire courage in others. Equally and self-evidently, the cowardly discourages. Courage to stand up to bullies and injustice. Courage to seize the day. Courage to go the extra mile.

Some organizations have "courage" as a competency. As something they select in others. Possibly as something they think or hope they can develop or train. But it is important to distinguish between various types of courage.

Interpersonal courage – This is perhaps the most important type in business. At the management level it involves confronting poor performers. It means standing up to bullies. Every organization has a number of well-dug-in underperformers who have learnt a range of ways to avoid being chastised or removed from their jobs. They consult doctors, lawyers, HR specialists and union representatives to obtain notes, letters and other threatening mechanisms to excuse their poor performance. Some simply do emotional outbursts, accusing managers of a range of "isms" that are likely to put off anyone. Racism, sexism, ageism, heightism but never performanceism. Or they may try the phobias: homophobia, xenophobia, Islamophobia.

It is easier to back down, back away from these individuals, than confront them. But left alone they grow. They are joined by others who learn the skills, the attitudes and devious devices of the aggressive underperformer.

The single best predictor of managers' success in some organizations is their willingness, ability and courage to confront others assertively and constructively. Often it is big, strong, chaps who find this form of courage the hardest.

It's also the courage to deliver other difficult messages. Ever had the body odor problem and tried to let the offender know that? Or dismissed the older worker who is no longer really up to it? Not nice. Not easy. It takes a mixture of skill and courage.

Risk-taking courage – Business is about taking calculated risks. This involves analysis first, courage second. Nearly every successful entrepreneur failed several times before they succeeded. They took a punt, invested a lot – and failed.

Some people are simply too cautious to really succeed. They may suffer analysis paralysis. They worry about failure; they commit insufficient resources or energy to ensure success.

The British are said to be brilliant inventors but hopeless exploiters of these ideas. Scientists are often cautious-analytic people.

There are many reasons why businesses fail or simply fail to thrive. One is that senior managers can't or won't take risks with new products, ideas, markets. They wait for others, who always win in the end. Risk-taking is part intellectual, part emotional. It's acting on imperfect information, carefully weighed. The cautious and cowardly wait too long until they are certain, and that, in business, is too late.

Moral courage – Although the very idea of business ethics is essentially oxymoronic for many, all managers need to know the difference between right and wrong. Of course things can be fudged, as in the famous phrase "tax evoision." And yes, there are different moral codes. There is also that gray area between what is called the spirit and the letter of the law.

Senior managers have powers and privileges and with them come temptations. Temptations that are so easy to give in to. Promoting favorites or lovers; fudging documents or announcements; telling half-truths; increasing one's own salary. The *New York Times* recently printed a list of CEOs who were in prison. All had seriously transgressed the law. Were they psychopathic, immoral imbeciles or simply not courageous enough to stand up to moral temptation?

There are many pressures on businesspeople sometimes dictated by what they see as demanding and greedy shareholders. And sometimes they have to resist the pressures to do something immoral (even amoral) or illegal to save their skin or make them look good.

Moral courage is admirable and rare. And not to be confused with self-righteous fundamentalism in the marketplace, or pompous trumpeting about ethical this and that. That is often little more than cleverly exploiting the current zeitgeist to save the planet.

Physical courage – Many great leaders have shown immense physical courage and not only military leaders. Explorers like Hillary and Shackleton are good examples. Space travelers, doctors in wars, even politicians have stood up to the unknown, the hostile crowd, the aggressive bully.

Physical courage is about endurance and defiance. It is about pushing yourself when you feel there is little left to give. It's about leading from the front.

So courage is multifaceted. Much exists to discourage us from being courageous, from health and safety obsessionality to fear of failure and looking foolish. But from a management perspective it seems almost foolhardy not to look out for signs of all four facets in our top managers and leaders.

Corporate police

Whether in the manufacturing or the service sector the history of most companies is much the same, save in a few respects. It could be a firm of engineers or lawyers; a restaurant owner or baker; a widget manufacturer or a hairdresser. The story goes like this.

The founder starts off with a few people, often family, performing multiple tasks. The enterprise flourishes so they expand to another site and/or grow the business at home. The founder wants to ensure that his successful formula is replicated so systems are introduced to copy the original one. It's a sort of internal franchising.

Soon they need managers of the growing numbers of people to organize and coordinate plans. Then they find they need not a part-time book-keeper, but a full-time accountant. And then a small group. They also need an HR person to do payroll and the legal stuff.

At what point and for what purpose small enterprises hire different specialists depends on many factors. Some resist for too long. They see certain functions as essentially a tax on the organization: a cost not a profit center. So they keep them lean and mean. Others invest more heavily.

Big organizations have in effect their own police force. Many organizations do, but they go under different names. There are the military police. Universities have them going under various charming names like Beadles or Bulldogs. Some call them internal security.

Really big organizations have some staff employed to look inward and assess the appropriate workings of the organization. They are usually found in one or other of the following departments: auditing, human resources, quality control and security. Their job is to maintain order and control to ensure processes and procedures are upheld.

There are corporate threats from inside and from outside. Thieves, con-artists, saboteurs, whistle-blowers are found inside and outside organizations. Some may have turned sour as a function of how they were managed, vengefully stealing goods or secrets, or telephoning the press with juicy tittle-tattle about the less than moral behavior of much-hated bosses. Others have deliberately sought employment in organizations because of the rich pickings that operate there.

The corporate police – your internal auditor, your quality controller – are much hated and lampooned. They are seen as the internal enemy, obsessional bureaucrats who slow everything down. They are taxing in all sorts of senses. They are humorless enforcers of petty, point-less laws and rules passed by EU characters with themselves too little to do.

So why bother to do more than the very minimum to comply with the law? Why invest so much in the internal monitoring? The answer is because it pays. Ask a Barings or Enron shareholder. The organizational police have the job of protecting the organization and its members; of monitoring; and of looking out for many kinds of deceitful and illegal behavior. They are there to catch the psychopath in the boardroom as well as the petty thief in stores. They are there to check up on the auditors. The question, of course, is who polices them.

All too frequently one reads reports of "little people" ripping literally millions from an organization over the years without anybody noticing. It happens in local government, the City and the high street. Incredulous outsiders ask how they could get away with it for so long. What procedures and processes are in place to stop this sort of thing? The answer of course is not enough.

You don't hear too much about the activities of internal auditors. It only makes bad PR. But pour a good glass of claret too much for one at a party and prepare to be amazed. Not by the petty fiddling of expenses but the really big stuff.

The anti-hierarchical, right-sizing 1980s and 1990s led to leaner, flat-ter, more free-form, faster-paced organizational structures, philosophies and environments. They were simplified, reprocessed. There were fewer controls, fewer checks and balances. It was more important to be innova-tive, adaptive, quick-to-market than tracking processes. There were fewer status-quo managers and more cage-rattlers.

Change and confusion are precisely the environments where the psy-chopath can thrive. Their callousness and insensitivity can look like boldness. Their eccentricity, their creativity and their impulsiveness just a proper sense of urgency. Businesses hire quickly. There is little time for HR to do all the oldfashioned, due-diligence stuff, checking up on the veracity of claims made on application forms.

Machines replaced some quality controls. Internal audit was slashed, cheaper security was outsourced to badly paid, bored workers who could neither pay attention nor speak much English. And guess what happened?

Little Mafiosi sects thrived; con-artists had a field-day; and thousands were spent on court cases.

The trick is to have enough well-trained and well-rewarded corporate police to service the particular purposes of the organization. Easier said than done. But a business case can easily be made to show they are a good investment.

Corruption at work

"Never underestimate," wrote Claude Cockburn, the Irish writer, "the effectiveness of a straight cash bribe." But when is a bribe a bribe or a thankyou or a present? And what of jumping up the waiting list because of a personal friendship? Or ensuring nepotistic appointment or promotion?

Backhanders, cronyism, favoritism – a long list of what are now called *counter-productive behaviors at work.* Why do they occur and what to do about them? Are they more common in service or in manufacturing industries? Why does corruption take different forms?

There are – and will remain – problems of definition. We are expedient, they are corrupt. I am pragmatic, she is unethical. For some it is easier to have quantitative rather than qualitative cutoff points. So "liberating" stationery worth around £30 is not a sin, but "half-inching" a laptop worth £450 is. So there are little "white" lies that don't count and big ones that do. Taking a "sickie" is another gray area. Is that stealing time, or doing as everybody else is doing?

What causes counterproductive work behaviors (CWBs)? There are lots of types of CWBs: pilfering, destruction, rule-breaking, disruptive practices, passive non-cooperation, misuse of facilities. Three types of factors are involved. The first is the most obvious. It's bad people – morally bad people. Bullies, psychopaths, perverts and the like. They harass, manipulate, cheat, steal and so on. They do exist; they are not good news; they were selection mistakes.

Paradoxically, bad people can do well in business for quite a time. Psychopaths can be very charming and persuasive; bullies can get things done. But for the most part they do get caught. And they don't account for that much of the problem.

Many managers support this "bad egg" theory. It might not absolve them from serious bad selection decisions but it does absolve them from the accusation of bad management. People act badly at work through greed, vanity, envy, ambition, love of excitement. They can be in senior or junior positions.

The second factor is poor management. People have clear expectations of what they expect from their boss. They develop a psychological contract – an emotion-laden concept that captures the nature of the exchange between worker and organization.

All workers are sensitive to unfairness, to bullying, blamestorming bosses. People leave managers, not organizations. A corrupt, lazy, ineffectual boss can easily be the primary cause of CWBs. People might steal or go absent, they might sabotage and are highly likely to bad-mouth.

Studies show the following typical causes of corrupt behavior. People are vengeful because they are passed over for promotion; promises are reneged upon; perks are removed. They feel their appraisals are unjust, their boss both demanding and rude, as well as self-serving, political and incompetent.

The sense of being unjustly dealt with, being abused or being ignored can soon lead to disillusion, resentment and thence revenge. Bad bosses are probably more common causes of corruption than bad employees.

The third factor is corporate culture: the well-established patterns of beliefs and behaviors that are in fact corrupt. Some people cheat at work because cheating is the norm. In their job they may be able to cheat customers, the taxman, the company. They may receive bribes – called tips, or favors or "thankyous." And the organization, or at least part of it, may well either turn a blind eye or even encourage it because it is an alternative source of pay.

Frustrated supervisors, unable to reward materially their hardworking staff, may quite simply put in place a system that provides rewards: stock may be removed and charged to customers; days off are approved; "fiddles" become the norm. So "sickies" become a perk of the job, as does finding one bottle of wine in ten corked.

Organizational culture can provoke loyalty or disloyalty. It can perpetuate an atmosphere of surveillance, suspicion and lack of trust. Employees may rely on ineffectual spin to cover up their inefficiency, even illegality.

Some corporate cultures do "squeaky clean" with regard to corruption. Others do spirit rather than letter of the law. Some do "blind eye." And others do crypto-Mafiosi.

Personal susceptibilities, incompetent managers and organizational culture together produce dysfunctional people in dysfunctional organizations. But it may also take something else: persuaders who push certain individuals over the limit. Competitors and criminals; family and friends; recruiters and journalists can tip people over the edge.

The amount of money lost through shrinkage in big firms is significant: well into seven figures. So corruption at work: a few wicked people, or a widespread malaise?

Courage and cowardice

To what extent is poor management a failure of courage? Courage to make tough decisions, take risks, deal with bullies, poor performers. Is the pusillanimous, contemptible timidity of ball-less managers a major cause of business failure?

But a failure of courage is quite different from trait-cowardice. The gutless, spineless wimp behaves consistently. Many, in times of crisis, confusion or great change simply seem paralyzed. Cognitively, emotionally, behaviorally frozen by fear and an inability to act.

So what then is courage? Why do some people have it and others not? Can it be learnt, trained and encouraged? Many writers have wrestled with definitions, trying to identify individual components. Some start with synonyms: bravery, endurance, fortitude, integrity and vitality. Others try to distil the essential properties of the courageous act:

- The person has free choice to act.
- They experience significant risk in doing so.
- They assess the risk as reasonable.
- The act has a worthy aim: justice, excellence and so on.
- The person proceeds despite fear.

Certainly there appear to be core components of the concept. First, a courageous act must be *deliberate and intended* – unconstrained, driven by reason and values. Next, there must be *substantial known risks*. Call them risks, difficulties or dangers. It means that the act of courage could end in anything from public humiliation to sacking, imprisonment or death. The actor must understand the risks probabilistically, but nevertheless do the deed.

Then there is the *noble cause*. This distinguishes similar acts from being selfish, reckless or pointless. Whistle-blowers are courageous if they aim to report harmful, illegal or unethical behavior. They are not courageous if this act is motivated primarily by revenge, greed or publicity.

Finally there is the *conquering of fear*. Situations calling for courage – both physical and moral – involve fear. Courageous people conquer their fears.

So the brave courageous manager is focused and selfless; fearless and honorable, dedicated and self-sacrificial.

The question then becomes: Why are some individuals more coura-geous than others? Can you select for trait-courage in managers? Can organizational courage be developed? Do some cultures produce people of courage while others do not?

Certainly there are noticeable differences in courage at work:

- *Interpersonal* courage in appraisals.
- *Moral* courage in dealing with various stakeholder or government groups.
- *Risk-taking* courage in investing heavily in new products or plant.
- *Physical* courage in standing up to hostile crowds.

Courage requires *assertiveness*. It also requires a *conscience*. Courageous people should be *stable* rather than neurotic. *Agreeable* rather than Machi-avellian. They need to be *bright enough* to understand the risks. These things can be selected for.

But perhaps it is easier and better to deal with courage on the orga-nizational (and societal) level. Setting examples and praising instances of managerial courage are clearly a good idea. Stories and heroes need to have the theme of courage.

Many of us were brought up with Scott and Shackleton as real heroes. Theirs were wonderful tales of attempting to conquer adversity, of personal sacrifice, of physical hardship.

Know any good managerial courage yarns? There are a few in the whistleblower tradition. Perhaps the greatest issue is not the risk assess-ment or even the conquering of fear part, but the noble cause. Somehow maintaining the share price doesn't seem as noble as saving one's colleagues or fighting for democracy.

A lot of business courage is about morality: seeing things to be wrong, unjust or illegal and then doing something about it. This may involve the wrath, ire and revenge of the board, or even imprisonment in foreign countries.

Courage goes with conscience. It goes with right and wrong and noble causes. It is a way of cutting the knot.

Making a "career-limiting" comment or move is a polite way of saying it doesn't pay to say or do certain things. How about asking candidates to give examples of:

- The last time they saw a good example of courage at work.
- The last time they acted courageously.
- What, in their experience, fosters or inhibits managerial courage.

We seem to have forgotten some of the old adages – "Service above self," "Play up, play up and play the game." We sneer at Victorian sentimentality and literature. But we are pretty grateful for our well-selected and trained troops whose courage is tested every day. Talk to them about managerial courage and your average manager may learn a thing or two.

Disagreeable leaders

Does it pay to be agreeable at work? The agreeable person is altruistic, trusting and straightforward. Warm, gentle, generous, kind and tolerant. Agreeable people tend also to be modest and tender-minded. They are friendly and soft-hearted. They believe in caring and sharing; coaching and counseling; forgiveness and redemption.

Disagreeable people, on the other hand, are suspicious and wary; hard-hearted and demanding; assertive, even aggressive; self-confident, even arrogant.

Few people want to be thought of as disagreeable but does it pay? The data suggest, perhaps paradoxically, that successful leaders tend to be, if anything, disagreeable. They have the ability, willingness and guts to "kick ass," "bite the bullet," "confront poor performers."

Effective leaders have identifiable characteristics:

- They act with integrity – they keep their word, they don't have favorites, they obey the law.
- They make good decisions – they are clear and decisive even under pressure.
- They are smart – creative, competent, with comprehensive knowledge.
- They have an inspirational vision – that of organizational (as opposed to exclusively personal) success.
- They are hard-working – conscientious, diligent, involved.

But what if they are cold, impersonal, hard taskmasters? This is different from being feared or actively disliked. It's about being frosty, perhaps distant.

There are essentially two issues here. The *first* is the nature of the motivation of the staff. The *second* is whether a softy can confront poor performance. Some jobs offer relatively little choice of whom you work for and how hard you have to work. If you are a professional footballer there is a clear rank order of where you may want to play and little choice of your fitness regime.

If there is scarcity of options the providers can do as they wish. Indeed this is a major reason why there is such opposition to monopolies. If you have to get a qualification, or join a society or undergo a specific apprentice-ship and there is no choice, or a very limited one, the concept of customer responsiveness goes out the window. And leaders need not be particularly charming.

So the first issue is about defection. The bottom line is that agreeable-ness is not necessarily a requirement of good leadership in situations where followers cannot easily defect.

But the second issue is one of skill. Let us assume that agreeableness is essentially a personality trait. You can't learn to be agreeable, but you can learn agreeable behaviors and tactics. So there are charm schools, emotional intelligence classes and many kinds of skill-based programs that are intended to teach the less agreeable to *appear* more agreeable.

Yet that is not really the problem. The problem lies in being "Mr Nice Guy." Agreeable managers tend to be too kind, too softy, too forgiving. They avoid giving people a dressing down when it would actually be appro-priate. They tend not to fire the incompetent, but send them on training courses and give them second chances. They turn a blind eye to excessive absenteeism and to justify their position.

No wonder agreeableness does not go with business success in a rough, tough, competitive world. But just as disagreeable managers can be taught strategies to make them behaviorally more empathic, so agreeable man-agers can be taught how to confront and how to give negative feedback without feeling guilty, inadequate or harsh.

The F-words are important in management: fairness, feedback, follow-ups. Perhaps the most important is fairness. All staff want their bosses to be fair. And neither the strongly agreeable nor the strongly disagreeable manager is thought of as fair. Paradoxically, agreeable managers – the softies of the business world – are often thought of as less fair because they refrain from confrontation. Disagreeable chaps may be cold and hard-hearted, but that does not mean they are necessarily unfair.

So there could be a cost to having a warm, empathic and generous man-ager. Unless, of course, they have been taught the skills of confrontation and giving negative feedback.

Disengagement levels

Customers, staff engagement levels and profits are in decline. Competitors, taxation and wage levels are on the increase. The exhausted CEO seems to have no other tricks hidden in his toolkit. An all-too-familiar scenario?

In the company as a whole – and for a long time now – the music and the words don't match. Everybody knows that talk of change and positive progress are little more than illusions. Senior managers are devising their escape plans. Some are simply burnt out with change fatigue.

Senior staff are either hyperactive with frenzied neurotic attempts to find and implement magic bullets at all costs, or hypoactive: moving and thinking like sloths or wombats oblivious to the crises around them.

So how to re-engage? How to bring meaning and joy back to a company? Should one simply "up stumps," or are things really recoverable? There are lots of reasons that companies fail: poor marketing, planning, or location; cash flow problems; lack of finance; failure to exploit and embrace new technology. Some are more easily correctable than others. But manager problems are addressable. There is no doubt that management style has an impact on corporate culture which, in turn, influences productivity. Purging managers at all levels might backfire. The trick is teaching them some fundamental skills; changing their outlook; resetting their thinking and practice.

People are engaged when they find their work meaningful; when they have some autonomy in the way they work and when they receive regular accurate feedback on how they are performing. Most of all where they have some control over their working lives.

Some jobs are inherently more "meaningful" than others. Compare a nurse with a parking attendant or a teacher with a sales clerk. But each job has its function and its place. The assembly plant worker, the lollipop lady, the security guard are doing useful jobs. It behoves management to communicate this message regularly and clearly. To be alienated at work is to find work meaningless, to feel powerless and to feel rudderless.

People need some sense of control at work: ideally how, when and why they work. Some jobs offer more control than others. People on shift work swap shifts, which can be a major perk.

We know that stress at work is a function of three things. *First*, where demands (on time, energy, concentration, skills) exceed supply, too often. *Second*, where one has no control or autonomy over most aspects of working conditions. *Third*, if one is a nervous type.

But lack of stress does not mean full of energy and optimism. A person can disengage from a previously unstressful and fulfilling job. People have an acute sense of injustice at work. They deeply resent promises broken and favoritism. They shred and burn their psychological contract if they detect dishonesty, corruption or speaking with forked tongues.

But all of these are what psychologists used to call hygiene factors. All they do is prevent disengagement, alienation and that long string of behavioral consequences from absenteeism to theft.

Getting all the conditions right still won't ensure engagement. Certainly some factors help. Some jobs are more intrinsically motivating than others. Some people are more positive, optimistic, more gung-ho than others.

But there remains the issue of morale. All good leaders know that one of the crucial aspects of the job is mood regulation. They need, regularly, to celebrate success. They need to be generous with praise. They need to publicly, openly, and regularly support their staff. They need to show pride, not so much in themselves, but in their staff and their brand.

And they need to do the vision inspiration stuff, the New Jerusalem message. You engage both heart and head. But it's an unstable compound which takes a lot of nurturing.

Dress for success

"Clothes maketh the man." Or "You can't make a silk purse out of a sow's ear." To what extent does gear make a difference in sales? Are you more likely to believe in, buy from, indeed even be more product-satisfied as a function of the attire of sales staff?

Everyone in the sales business has been brought up on a mantra of *presentation.* Restaurant owners know that "we eat with our eyes." It seems plate arrangement is at least as important as raw ingredients. Equally the *packaging* is as important as the product, particularly in upmarket luxury goods like perfume.

Grocery stores invest heavily in making the shelves look orderly and full. Car showrooms are the result of much designer time and money. Malls and large department stores are carefully planned to guide, enthral and impress the customer. Lighting, music, mirrors, smells and signage all try to combine to maximize that simple single factor – increasing the sales.

Similarly, sales staff are trained to give the right impression. They may be rigorously or casually scripted to say particular phrases. They may equally have gone on various body language courses to make them both more perceptive and self-aware. What is the customer's body language saying to you, and vice versa?

But what are the rules for and effects of attire? Surely it has some impact? The first solution is the uniform. Some organizations rejoice in smart uniform. Airlines probably come top of the uniform league outside the military. Not only are they smart and fashionable but staff have to follow rigorous rules about such aspects as how they wear their hair and how much jewelry they are allowed; there are even rules about fingernail length and color.

Various organizations that gave up uniforms such as rail companies have reintroduced them. For the customer uniforms have many advantages. *First*, staff are easily identifiable. It's often embarrassing, in a bookshop for instance, having to ask three people (customers) before you find the person you are after (actual staff). *Second*, you can (usually) tell the person in charge. That is, uniforms give a sign of rank. *Third*, they can reinforce the brand. They can wear the logo and literally make the brand come alive.

Some uniforms are as much functional as fashionable. They are meant to improve hygiene or safety or whatever. Some are frankly comical, like the daft Dickensian outfits worn by those tip-hungry guys outside hotels eager to hail a taxi for you.

On the other hand some organizations either have dated, tacky uniforms that few could wear with pride or let staff add idiosyncratic touches and additions. Fast-food outlets often have semi-uniformed staff.

Read a child's story book and you can see everyone on the high street seems to have an outfit. The baker with his tall hat; the butcher with his apron; the tailor with his tape measure.

Many people have come to expect their professionals dressed in a particular way. A few years ago the *British Journal of Psychiatry* published a paper showing six or so pictures of doctors. They went from the formal tie, white coat, and stethoscope slung around the neck to the completely dressed-down doctor in "smart casual" wear. What did people prefer? You guessed it – not too formal, but most still liked the professional medical look with white coat.

Various people at work might have attire choice; the clergy to wear dog-collars; private nurses to wear uniforms. There is also choice within the uniform. Sometimes there are uniforms for special occasions. Most people like to see a vice-chancellor in full finery for a graduation or undertakers in old-fashioned clothes for a funeral.

But does it make a difference in a department store? Why do photo-copier repair men arrive in short-sleeved shirts? Can you tell the quality (and cost) of a hotel by the smartness of the staff, from the receptionists in the lobby through to the humble chambermaid, forever fluffing up pillows and dispersing "nite-nite chokkies?"

It's not so difficult to design an experiment to test the power of dress. Choose a service sector: it could be a restaurant, or a hairdresser's, or some such. For three weeks vary nothing but the dress of the staff: same people, same service, same costs. In week one it's business as usual. In week two it's idiosyncratic-smart: staff can have personal choice, but are required to go from casual to smart with perhaps flair and fashion. In week three they are in uniforms. Ideally you use different restaurants, different types of uniforms and so on at the same time to ensure greater generalizability of finding. And what do you measure? Customer feedback forms, tips, intentions to return.

Yes, location is important, as is quality and cost. But for more and more people in a service industry eager to obtain competitive advantage, it may be worthwhile checking out the subtle but persuasive effects of dress. They used to say "If you want to get ahead, get a hat." Perhaps that applies to all apparel: dress for success.

Evolutionary consumption

The Darwinians are now masters of the universe. Their handsomest and cleverest spokesman is Richard Dawkins who, like Nietzsche, found God dead. Or more precisely that he never existed.

Evolutionary explanations are in. They are powerful, alluring and popular. Nowhere more so than of course issues around mating. Evolutionary psychologists have taken a particular interest in the whole business of physical attraction. They speak in code. What is feminine beauty? Answer: a BMI of 22, a WHR of .7 and LTR of 1.2. Huh? That's body mass index (lean and mean), waist-to-hip ratio (curvy), and leg-to-torso ratio (leggy).

And what do women want? GSOH, an inverted triangle and a thick billfold. *Good sense of humor* is code for intelligence, inverted triangle is broad shoulders and trim waist and the wallet is pretty obvious.

We are programmed to spot good breeders. Men want feminine women, women want men who will make clever, fit babies and have the money to support them.

What a wealth of causes and philosophies Darwin has served, from imperialism to nationalism, from work ethic to consumerism, from mysticism to Marxism, from competition to cooperation, individualism to collectivism etc. His useful employment seems to stop only at the limits of the human imagination, while even in the evolutionist camp there are massive differences. They argue that conspicuous consumption is primarily about sexual signaling. So young men drive down the cruising strip in expensive sports cars belting out loud rhythmic music, while young women pose in provocative (read skimpy) attire. The fashion business looks for tall models who are symmetrical. They like smooth skin and hair, signaling health, and a deep voice for the male models.

It is no puzzle to the Darwinians why women spend so much time and money on appearance-enhancing products. Cosmetics, plastic surgery, sun beds, fashion items are there to accentuate youth and beauty. These products exist simply because of the evolved preferences of men.

Men signal status in clothes and accessories. The 45-year-old man buys a red sports car, his wife has a facelift. They are both responding exactly as the Darwinians would predict. They argue that the sexes differ today as a result of facing (in evolutionary history) different adaptive problems (like mating). Where they faced the same problem, like finding enough to eat, they don't differ. So the sexes share equally a love of rich food.

Evolutionary psychologists cite magazine ads to justify their case. Take any glossies clearly aimed at women versus those at men. Do a content analysis of the advertisements. Note also the things that are universal (and therefore not modified much by culture learning) like the shape of female models. And, if you are up for it, look at soft-porn, "top shelf" magazines. They contain, as the evolutionists argue, "universal visual semiotics," because of all males' mating preferences.

Physiologists have shown that specific biological processes like the menstrual cycle, testosterone levels and even hunger relate to consumption. When women are most fertile they are more likely to buy sex-specific products (like lingerie and cosmetics), more likely to reduce their calorific intake (not to be distracted from the competitive drive of mating), more likely to cheat on their partner for a physically superior male, more attracted to the square-jawed masculine look.

And all-you-can-eat buffets, or huge, stocked-up grocery stores appeal to the universal need for calorific hoarding. The Darwinians note how evolutionary forces have encouraged the dark side of consumption. The gambling, sex, slimming and tanning industries owe their existence to our caveman past. Indeed people with problem addictions – gambling and sex – often show co-morbidity as the theorists predict. Gambling is a means of acquiring resources easily while sex addiction is a proclivity for short-term mating opportunities. Women who are prone to eating disorders are more likely to sunbathe excessively.

Most sunbathers are single, young females who trade off (quite knowingly) short-term benefits (mate attraction) with long-term consequences (skin cancer). The Darwinians say you don't persuade people by giving them information about future health consequence, but rather about short-term gains. So warn sunbathers that skin blisters and acne occur. Warn young (male) smokers that smoking leads to erectile dysfunction and you might be more successful.

And most dodgy financial-deal-making, risk-seeking people are young men. Men are motivated to acquire resources and status to increase their mating attractiveness. That is, old, withered multimillionaires find no problem in acquiring a sexy mate fifty years their junior. Young men will compete aggressively and sometimes illegally for resources.

The evolutionary account looks at "ultimate rather than proximate" explanations of all human behavior from consumption to leisure time activities. So they disagree strongly with all sorts, from economists to feminists. Economists believe we make consumer decisions based on utility maximization. Tosh – well, at least in so far as people's behavior is adaptive, say Darwinians. The ultimate consumer mechanism is *inclusive fitness:* passing on good genes. Irrational conspicuous consumption is simply about signaling financial resources.

Perhaps it is no wonder that those popular books about people from different planets sell well. They are essentially about evolutionary explanations. There are others, too, about why boys don't cry and women do the dishes.

Management gurus have attempted to apply evolutionary psychology to the workplace with some success. Isn't it about time the marketing strategists climbed on board? They might just get a shot of the USP they all seek in understanding how to position a brand for optimal consumption.

Executive education excess

Charge what the market will bear. Good advice. Rarely expect much of a correlation between quality and price, package and promise.

Blind tastings make for sober findings. Magazines frequently conduct expert blind tastings of everything from champagne to potato crisps, olive oil to Bath Oliver biscuits, sherry to shortbread. And there are nearly always surprises. Grocery store own-brands receive five stars while snootily marketed, organically sourced, fair-trade, by-appointment brands receive one or no stars.

Blind tasters concentrate on core contents. These tests blinds them to brand packaging and proposition. More importantly, they conduct their comparisons on specific, preordained criteria.

Unlike food and wines, some experiences can't be "blinded," but they can be compared. Thus doctors can be rated according to their bedside/consultation manner, their perceptiveness, or their diagnostic accuracy. Equally lawyers, teachers and all other professionals can be appraised. But the tradition has been, perhaps correctly, to measure some output variable. So schools are measured by exam success, by truancy rates, and by staff and pupil turnover.

But how to measure services that are really all content? The usual criteria are a very misleading trilogy: advertising, price and reputation.

Imagine the HR training or development manager with a hefty budget for executive education (exec-ed). The new CEO believes in it and was perhaps the happy graduate of a course that promoted fresh thinking. He or she may have bonded with a group from the company or made new friends. Or the new CEO may simply believe that the senior managers are too insular, uninformed, out of date in their thinking.

So the training manager is tasked with finding the best exec-ed course. There certainly is no scarcity. Indeed a bewildering array of short, medium, long courses; classroom-based vs. outdoor or action-learning; some leading to a degree or diploma; some at home and some abroad; some specialist, some generalist. It's a competitive market because it is a lucrative market.

So how to choose? Best start with the desired output. What precisely could the purchasers expect? Is the course in and of itself simply a reward for good behavior? A time-out? A trophy to be discussed at dinner parties? No

ROI then? Or are there to be psychological, even behavioral consequences? Is it meant to be an enriching or (God forbid) a life-changing experience?

Are those on the course going alone or in groups? From whom are they meant to learn: the educators, each other or others on the course? Do you get better value from four one-week courses than one four-week course? Is the money to be spent proportional to rank or status or inversely proportional? Do people 55 years old and over really benefit in any way from those courses?

So start with a clear set of realistic goals. The emphasis is on realism. Then where to go. What about prestige: Harvard or London Business School? What evidence that they do a better job than East Cheam University that used to be a polytechnical college? Surely there is a clear relationship between prestige, price and quality? Doubtful. A better or at least a richer class of participant surely, but a better experience?

And what about that overcrowded second division? Those business schools in lovely settings where there may be more gardeners than professors. Are they not exec-ed factories rather like holiday hotels? As one group leaves another enters. The logo and title change but they all get the core product which seems to work. Executive sheep-dip. No bad thing for those who have little experience of management education?

Many executives love the idea, if not the whole experience, of the company-based, company-financed Master of Business Administration (MBA). Pick up a sexy degree at the company expense. But it's a long and very tiring slog. The MBA managers are tired and overstretched. Their marriages fail. They become stressed and ill. And soon after they graduate their new whiff of entrepreneurship sees them resigning and starting their own business.

The moral of the story: be clear what you want and expect from exec-ed. Don't assume reputation and marketing are enough to base your choice on. Prepare a set of questions you want answered by the execed deliverers (How do they measure success? How do they customize courses?). And, as always, *caveat emptor*.

Fear and greed

Perhaps it was all that 1980s and 1990s time-wasting nonsense about vision and mission statements that led people to be bored by the concept of values at work. Remember the hours (and therefore money) spent on coming up with "inspirational and aspirational" twaddle about "best in the world," "delighting customers" and "ethical policies"?

They were all supposed to be different but were all the same. Indeed they should have been. They were what every company's mission/vision/purpose statement should be. "To provide continuous maximum return for shareholders." All right, stakeholders if you must, but that is a slippery slide.

Another 1980s revival seemed to deflect attention from the values theme: business ethics. Courses, journals, books flourished as it was advocated in a guru-like, data-free sort of way that ethical companies were actually more profitable. Perhaps. And now we see a rush to be ethical banks, have ethical investments and so on. There is the oxymoronic "fair trade" concept which stretches nicely to become a convenient but meaningless strapline. What is unfair trade? If you don't have the fair trade label are you trading unfairly and exploitatively?

So "work values" were put aside. Pity, because they help explain and predict. Values are quite simply a person's most important and enduring beliefs. They can be grouped into a reasonably parsimonious number (around a dozen) and quite easily measured. People don't fake too much on value measures. Also, friends and colleagues can very accurately list a person's most important values: that is, they are easily inferred from behavior.

Why are the values of managers important? Because values in part determine many things:

- What data (information) they really pay attention to, or ignore.
- What problems they see as critical vs. trivial.
- Where they invest time, money and effort in the business.
- How they consistently solve problems.
- How they evaluate the effectiveness of all solutions.
- How they implicitly or explicitly select others and run teams.

The value-driven, consistent behaviors of top leaders create the corporate culture, which is itself little more than implicit beliefs and norms of behavior.

We seek out, like and marry people who see the world as we do; who share our (most fundamental) values. Hence the idea of fit – an alignment between personal, group and corporate values. However able and motivated a person might be, if a manager has a conflict of values he or she soon leaves the organization.

One way to look at business values is that of tension between opposites. This runs into problems because it is not always clear what they are. The opposite of altruism is? The opposite of security is? It's more reliable to look at a whole *profile* of values than scores on each dimension So one value that really drives people is *recognition* or, in excess, vanity. It's about wanting to be noticed, admired, deferred to. It's about appearing in *Hello!* magazine, being interviewed by Oprah or Richard and Judy, about a knighthood and so on. Another is *power* – wanting to have an impact, create a legacy, influence the way things are done.

Thus people in the caring and health professions endorse the beliefs and behaviors of the value *altruism* (helping others), while those in the City endorse classic *commercial* values of financial success, growth and exploiting business opportunities. People in fashion, art, architecture espouse *aesthetic* values of beauty, form, style. Some military, religious and educational leaders are driven by *traditional* values such as self-discipline, the family unit, respect for authority.

Values lead to failure and success. People can be profiled by their values. People in business tend to be high on *power* and *commerce* and low on *security*. These are associated with those crucial ingredients for business success, energy, drive, risk-taking. But what if they are also associated with strong *recognition* and low *altruism*? These are the makings of greed, selfishness and rule-bending.

"Greed is good" was a 1980s mantra. You are still allowed to say this in the confines of your own boardroom with those who share those values. Nothing wrong with that? Well it depends. Think of a manager high on *hedonism* and low on *affiliation*: a pleasure-seeking egocentric.

Some values don't seem to go with business success. Valuing altruism, security and tradition seem antithetical to the cut-and-thrust world of the boardroom. Valuing hedonism, power and recognition on the other hand might lead to some pretty unwise long-term decision-making.

It pays to explore a manager's values. And question one's own periodically. Too much value homogeneity in the boardroom often leads to groupthink and bad decisions. Thinking about how people with different values from one's own approach issues may help decision-making. But then your values also dictate whether you like to brook opposition and think through questions from different points of view.

Feedback phobia?

Name one organization where people are generally happy with their appraisal process. Name one organization where, if they indeed have a process, it has not been chopped and changed as disillusionment, anger and sabotage have set in. Name one senior person who doesn't want personal feedback. And one who actually enjoys delivering it.

The concept of performance appraisal is based on some important and simple principles: people want to know how they are doing; managers and supervisors are able and willing to give performance feedback; accurate, timely feedback improves performance. True? So whence the cynicism, dread and distrust around the whole appraisal process?

The consequences of not having feedback can really be very serious. Is the real reason simple then? Give them positive feedback and you unrealistically raise expectations of salary increase, promotion and the like. Give them negative feedback and you get tears and allegations of aggression, bullying and harassment. Tribunals and lawyers follow from telling feckless, lazy, incompetent people that they are precisely that!

So let's start again. Do we always want feedback? Answer: yes – if it's positive, yes – if it fits in with our picture of our efforts and abilities. No – if it's negative, very strongly no – if it's not constructive, in the sense that it does not suggest and support alternative behaviors. Feedback can be bland, overwhelmingly complex, or carefully coded to make it worthless to the individual.

Point two: aren't managers able and willing to give feedback? Answer: no – if they don't have, keep or understand performance data; don't know how to conduct appraisals; don't have any control over how the performance ratings are used; or are scared of confronting poorly performing employees.

Third, does the feedback always produce positive changes? Answer? Sometimes. Depending. It all depends on two things. First, is it focused on personal characteristics, or task behaviors? The former often lead to worse performance. Second, is it specifically behavioral with a description of what is wanted and what is not? Tell people not what they do wrong, but what (in detail) they should do and you should get an improvement.

Of course much depends on the purpose of feedback ratings. Are they "administrative," in the sense that they are to inform salary, promotional and other decisions? Are they "developmental" in the sense that they are meant to inform overall training or are they "performance-oriented" in the sense that they are aimed at maintaining or changing very specific performances?

It seems there are two general categories of factors that influence the willingness to give and receive feedback: the characteristics of the people involved and the particular organizations.

Seven personal characteristics have been shown to relate to feedback exchange:

- Demographics: females seem more happy to act on feedback than males. Also people from less egalitarian and collectivist cultures seem happier to receive and do something about feedback.
- Personality: stable, agreeable, conscientious people give and receive feedback more enthusiastically.
- Performance level: by and large, better performers deal more in feedback. Some seek feedback more when they are underperforming, but that depends on the job and their motivations.
- Relationships: no surprise here. The better the relationship between rater and rated the more feedback is sought and used.
- The rater's emotions: this means how hot or cool is the way the feedback is delivered. Show negative emotions when giving negative feedback and the point of the activity is lost.
- Impression management: both the rater and rated can play games, put on roles. One can play therapist–patient; wise-elder–new-kid-on-the-block; ego-enhancement; job focus and so on. Being job focused is best, obviously.
- Supervisor commitment and engagement: happy bosses give more lenient ratings and *vice versa*. The pissed-off, political survivor uses and abuses the system for specific ends.
- Managers who trust the process give to their staff and receive better appraisals from their boss.

Inevitably appraisal works better in some organizations than in others. Organizations with higher morale, better overall performance, stronger systems and less politics are better, more frequent and happier users of feedback. Much depends on perceptions of the point of using feedback systems – how fair, open, honest they were.

Some organizations go in for 360-degree or multi-source feedback in a big way. That involves being rated by superiors, peers, subordinates and clients as well as self. It's meant to increase awareness and facilitate development. The trouble is that mostly the feedback is inconsistent and unclear. Why are the ratings so different; what should one do with it? It's like advice: you are not always sure what to do.

But surely to be in a feedbackless world is a nightmare? To know how you're doing and how to do it better must be good for the individual and the organization. People need to be taught to give detailed and objective feedback. But there is a gain/pain calculation to be made. Are all the ducking and weaving, game-playing and political shenanigans worth it?

Can we help people make accurate and fair self-assessments? Of course – but as ever it depends on what they are used for. Most of us want to know how we are (really) doing and improve. But we are not as closely managed as we once were and may have to find different ways of getting and giving feedback.

Full-glass optimism

Think of two incidences in the last three years/at college/at school where you had a major success or a major failure. Describe these. Now explain the cause. Was it something about you yourself, or the situation you were in? Is the cause pretty consistent and stable or highly variable? Third, does the cause have a major impact on all aspects of your life or is it really very confined to very specific situations?

So maybe you failed your driving test? Cause – mixture of incompetent instructor and bastard examiner? So it was about them, not you. And it's not stable – you can at least sack the former and hope you don't get the latter. And frankly it is not that important. But what if you thought the cause was your "nerves"? You perform badly under observation and examination conditions and always have. So nerves blighted your educational career. And had a significant impact on your life.

This is a good way to begin a sales selection interview. Why? It's attempting to get at a person's attribution style, which is a clear indicator of whether they are an optimist or a pessimist. And why is that important? Simple: not only are optimists healthier and happier, but they sell more. They bounce back from adversity. They set themselves higher targets. Optimism is self-fulfilling.

Anyone who has been to a sales and marketing conference knows about infectious optimism. Baden-Powell implored his followers to kick the "im" from impossible because he knew it was good for them. Successful sales people don't believe in luck, they make their own luck.

But to get back to the test. The idea is to get people to attribute the causes of their success and failure. Start by examining their nominated incident. How serious or trivial is it? How easy was it to decide on an example from success and failure? How much impression management is in it damning with faint praise or making the failure a success in disguise?

You may ask them to list a few more incidences, or be specific saying "when you actually failed a test or exam," "when you received an extremely positive annual appraisal" or "when you failed to be elected as a prefect."

Having got your incidents both positive and negative, the trick is to assess internality and externality. Who was the cause? Homer Simpson always says "I blame society." There is a whole generation now well schooled in the darker attribution arts. They failed geography because of the teacher; they passed math because of their ability. Psychologists say the pattern is healthy if indeed it is located in reality. There are bad, uninspiring, incompetent teachers. They lead to bewildered, demotivated pupils who tend never to pursue the discipline. But it is highly unlikely any individual experiences a long string of poor math teachers.

To blame others consistently for personal failure is a very bad sign. It represents a failure to take responsibility, to have sufficient self-insight, to have realistic expectations.

The second issue refers to the stability of causes. Some things are harder, if not impossible to change. You can't do much about your intelligence or height. You can do something, however, about your weight.

So if you believe the cause of your success is about the essence of you – all well and good. If you believe it's temporary that too may be OK as long as you know how to repeat it. But if you believe the cause of your failure is immutable, essential, fundamental issues, then you have problems.

And finally there is extension. That is, what are the extended consequences of the problem? If the supposed cause is such that it may influence many aspects of your life, it must be taken seriously. If it's positive – great. Being bright is a good example. It seems to affect everything in life, from education to longevity, from job success to personal relationships. Equally some characteristics may be a real handicap in all situations.

Some people seem to play to their strengths. They discover what those are and use them effectively. They know how to exploit their talents. And they are realistic about their success and their failure, treating those two imposters just the same.

Funny business

Marketing people want their advertisements to be remembered. Recall the brand then buy it. So what makes ads memorable? Does humor help or hinder the process? Simple question, but alas, as often, complicated answer.

Advertisers seem to think humor helps. Around a third of (all) media ads employ humor. Americans have costed this: over £20 billion is spent annually on humorous ads of all sorts. Of course what constitutes humor may be in dispute. After all, one man's humor is another's insult. There is visual vs. verbal humor. There is sexual, aggressive, or intellectual humor. There are gentle puns and clowning about. It's sure a funny thing, humor.

Advocates of humor in advertising claim it generates more attention, overcomes sales resistance, enhances the overall persuasiveness of the message. It involves and engages through charm, playfulness and "twinkle." It hits heart and mind. Funny-bone and cautious billfold.

But the detractors claim humor can all too often backfire. It draws attention more to the joke than the brand. It can really irritate on repetition. And there seem to be few universals about humor: it does not travel well. Different responses from men and women are engendered (geddit?) and there are cultural differences in what people find funny. The professionally offended can easily take umbrage. And so instead of pleasing the viewer you seriously annoy them.

But the use of humor in advertising involves more complex issues than these. At least three come to mind. First, is the humor relevant? Congruent? Does it fit with the product, the message and the surrounding material? There is a considerable amount of reasonably consistent evidence that incongruity attracts more attention. Things that don't fit stand out. Some ads seem to melt into the program, with one indistinguishably interwoven to the other. On the other hand, ads can be very different in style, mood and message. Memorable surely, but not always good news. Do funny ads work in programs about death and destruction, hurricanes and holocausts? But then, do any ads really work in those programs?

Next, and related to congruity, is expectancy. Does the viewer, listener or reader expect humor? Some products in some settings lead to an expectation of a joke. Alcohol and cars can be fine vehicles for humor. But life insurance, or pain relief pills?

And what of sense of humor or need for humor? Some people just don't get it. They seem puzzled by puns; angered by ambiguity; disgusted by *double entendres*. They don't do humor. Others like a good belly laugh; a shaggy-dog story; a series of quickfire jokes. While some have little need for humor, others really thrive on it.

A paper published by two American marketers (Kellaris and Cline 2007) describes the testing of some of these ideas using printed ads. Their interesting findings supported some previous research. They found that recall is damaged when humor is expected and seems conceptually related to the message. However, where it is not expected, humor helps recall. That is, for memory of the ad's brand unexpected information is superior to expected information and relevant information outperforms irrelevant information. Incongruity works best. We know this from other work on ads using drama, music or animation. So humor works where it is not expected.

They also found, quite unsurprisingly, that a person's need for humor or levity made a difference. Clearly some people seek out humor more than others. Their choice of books, television programs and live entertainment signals their enjoyment of humor. Humor in advertising works for the humorous and humor-seeking. That is, those (poor devils) characterized by a low need for (and hence appreciation of) humor are put off by humorous ads and remember the brand less clearly.

So unexpected relevant humor in ads helps recall in those people with a sense of humor. American organizations like Citibank and Budweiser beer have done clever, successful, expected, relevant humor ads. But others have failed badly by any way of measuring impact.

Advertisers have tried it all: sex, violence, car chases and humor. They all have the same aim but their results are dramatically different. Sex and violence don't sell: the jury is back. Humor can, but only for certain groups and certain conditions. Marketing people are not in the entertainment business. There is all the difference between being (mildly) amused by the ad, remembering the brand and later buying the product.

Reference

Kellaris, J. J. and Cline, T. W. (2007) "Humor and Ad Memorability: On the Contributions of Humor Expectancy, Relevancy, and Need for Humor," *Psychology and Marketing,* 24, 497–509.

Gossip is good for you

A gossip is a person who habitually reveals unusual, sensational, or hidden facts about other people: their motives, lifestyles, personal preferences. Gossip columnists are well-read, if not respected. To be labeled an "office gossip" is clearly pejorative. It is to be untrustworthy, to be "political" and to be potentially dangerous.

But evolutionary psychologists have tried to explain the pervasiveness and function of gossip in all groups. The word "gossip" is derived from the concept of a crony or kinsman. It is the chatty talk of peers. Gossip can be positive or negative, but scandal is exclusively negative. It is to bring into disrepute, to defame or to disgrace others.

Gossip is more than "small talk" and its function is usually more than simple entertainment. Gossips spread rumors. Rumors can initiate panic and riots. There are gossip enthusiasts: some who transmit, others who receive.

Gossip has three related functions:

- To remind group members of the group's real and important values and acceptable norms of behavior.
- To act as an effective deterrent to deviance.
- To punish those who transgress the norms.

Gossip has been described as order without law: how neighbors settle disputes. Notice how much of the script of soap operas is about gossip. Gossip can be about indirect aggression and about both establishing and strengthening sanctions.

So gossip is about uncovering cheats. It is also a tall-poppy-leveling mechanism for neutralizing those who get above their station or attempt to compromise the interests of the group. Gossip, along with ridicule and ostracism, is used in various groups to keep control.

But gossip is also used by Machiavellian individuals to attempt to further their own interests and reputation. Some use it to try to enhance their own success in social competition.

So what is gossip usually about?

- Control of resources – usually money, but often space and information flow.
- Sexual activity of all kinds.
- Alliances and political dealings between interested parties.
- Individual reputations for reliability and trustworthiness.

What is the difference between kidding, griping and whining? It is more than comparing, but how?

There have been numerous rather interesting studies on gossip. A number have confirmed some pretty obvious stuff. Thus people find gossip more interesting if it is (a) negative (scandals, misfortunes, misjudgment) or (b) about high-status (rather than low-status) people. People spread around positive gossip about allies (that is, promotions) but negative information about enemies.

Those with whom we prefer to share gossip tend to be same-sex, same-age-and-stage people. People gather in groups and enjoy a good gossip about the bosses, the customers and the shareholders they hate. Nothing like a bit of tittle-tattle about sexual infidelity or dysfunction, promiscuity, drunken behavior or drug/gambling/other addictions, or even major or minor theft!

Can gossip be positive? That is, can it involve how clever, talented, motivated or honest a person is? In this, can gossip serve one of its many functions by creating ideal models? It does not sound right. It sounds like PR, which is the very opposite of gossip. *Hello!* magazine seems the epitome of positive gossip.

Gossip is nearly always publicly denounced, but frequently socially valued. If you look at attitudes to gossips and gossiping there seem to be two clear factors. The first stresses the social value of gossip as a way of sharing information about others. There is also a moral factor which asks the difficult question about the truthfulness of gossip and the underhand way.

Does gossiping change much over the lifespan? Who gossips most? Men or women? When do children first begin to gossip? And what about? It's a very interesting topic, but is it worthy of research? Perhaps only doing the research can finally answer that question?

Certainly gossip at work is commonplace. Study a rumor and you find a social network of people "in the know." Call gossip "information communication" and you see why it can be important. You can't legislate against it or control it. Indeed attempts to manipulate it would probably backfire and quickly become the very stuff of gossip.

The Guinness Book of Management Records

The *Guinness Book of World Records* is a publishing success story. Further, its very existence leads to the most amazing, frequently amusing and sometimes utterly pointless feats of human endurance, stupidity and waste. What is it about people who swallow massive amounts of food or liquid in incredibly short periods, or who take part in marathon orgies of talking, or skipping or jumping to receive a few lines in the great book?

Records are divided into various sections. There are of course many sporting records, but there are also records in arts and the media. There is a section on the human body and one on travel and transport.

There is a group of human achievements, mostly to do with stamina or speed or reaction. There is a section on "The Youngest Person Ever To" and of course its equivalent called "Golden Oldies." There are short sections on consumption and wealth.

The book is brought out, updated every year. It is beautifully produced. And of course there are ever more categories, particularly of human endeavor. The publishers try hard to validate those activities and no doubt use serious resources to do so. Part of the brilliance of the product is that it is ever developing.

The core of the book remains much the same from year to year – the tallest man, the biggest volcano, the longest river. But there are always additions and changes that justify buying the update. A testament to its marketing success lies in the number of out-of-date copies that appear in goodwill stores. They lose value annually.

It's not clear whether the producers and verifiers need any help, but they do have some gaps in their books. Just as we have yet to find an anthology of business poetry, so there appears no section on business feats and achievements. Surely this situation needs to be rectified.

Can't we have a section on Business Records? Maybe it could, or should, be sponsored by charity. Imagine the companies lining up to get in – or not get in as the item dictates.

Perhaps the sections could be categorized on the criteria. The quickest/slowest, most/least expensive; heaviest/lightest; biggest/smallest; longest/shortest. Thus consider some possibilities.

Time

- Longest time working for an organization without receiving any form of feedback or appraisal.
- Longest time it took for the IT department to "get back to you" having experienced a computer failure.
- Quickest acceptance of a resignation proposal.
- Greatest absenteeism rate experienced by an organization.
- Longest time for a jacket to sit on a chairback, feigning presence while absent.
- Most time spent on personal internet business in one week.
- Shortest time between clicking "send" and the HR department demanding an explanation.
- Shortest time for a rumor to travel from the water cooler to the CEO's office.
- Most days spent out of the office by an executive voluntarily attending totally unnecessary training courses.
- Most time off ever taken to attend nativity plays/sports days/speech days/school visits, with corresponding record level of resentment measured in the child-free.
- Longest time between coffees ever recorded for the marketing director.
- Fastest time for this year's confidential bonus awards to be known to everyone.
- Number of times the same present has appeared in the Xmas "lucky dip."

Money

- Most expensive leadership development program.
- Most expensive logo rebranding exercise.
- Cheapest "wash bag" given to anyone by an airline.
- Highest-paid executive.
- Most money spent internet shopping during working hours.
- Most expensive bottle of wine ever bought by HR for someone's leaving party.
- Biggest fee ever quoted by a head-hunter without smiling.

Size

- Biggest office space inhabited by one (narcissistic) manager.
- Biggest packed lunch ever brought into work.

Number

- Highest number of business cards handed out at a networking forum.
- Highest number of sickies thrown by one person in a year.
- Highest number of cc's attached to an in-house email to cover sender's ass.
- Highest number of divorces filed after office Xmas party.
- Highest percentage of staff engaged in intra-office liaisons at one time.
- Lowest mileage ever required before the sales director can demand a new car.
- Maximum amount of eye contact ever recorded between a member of the IT department and another human being.
- Loudest laugh ever recorded in response to chairman's (feeble) jokes.
- Largest number of staff joining the mile-high club while away on business trips.
- Highest number of times the lawyers have been asked if the zeros on their check are correct.
- Largest number of cigarette butts left around "smokers" doorway outside the building.
- Largest number of body parts photographed on the photocopier at this year's office party.

Interpersonal

- Rudest email joke to have done the rounds before HR updated filters.
- Most physical damage ever inflicted by the firm handshakes of the sales department/visiting Americans.
- Maximum glare ever recorded from the bling of the sales department.
- Shortest skirt ever worn by Tracey in accounts.
- Largest number of chaps who have tried their luck with the good-looking girl on reception.
- Smallest number of staff names ever learnt by the CEO.

Of course, the events of recent months in the UK have prompted a new management record:

"The most confidential information ever lost by one government department," with several contenders for the top place. And the winner is . . .

Hand-me-down leadership

Clinicians say we parent as we were parented. If we were taught either implicitly or explicitly that showing emotions is somehow wrong and unacceptable we tend to repress them. Oddly this may occur for all emotions, not only anger, jealousy and sorrow, but also love, joy and compassion.

If our parents never argued or had big rows we grow up frightened by or quite unused to conflict. Hence some adults become massively conflict-averse, or learn to channel their fury into sarcasm, sulking or passive-aggressive spitefulness.

If children suffer rejection from one they loved, say by divorce, they may become commitment-phobes, unable to commit fully to anyone for fear of that terrible rejection.

And, of course, there is the darker side of physical and mental abuse in which the abused in turn becomes the abuser.

Some believe that our early authority figures – namely mummy and daddy – determine (at least in part) how we respond to all authority figures. There is a rich literature going back to the brilliant British psychiatrist John Bowlby on what is called attachment. It is just that: how healthily we are attached to our parents. The strength of this bond – particularly between mother and child – seems to have important consequences for life because it dictates how we bond with others.

But what does all this psychobabble have to do with business? The answer lies in the way to learn leadership. While bookstores groan under the weight of books on leadership they are not that extensively read. A surprising number of high-profile, successful leaders are happy to admit (nay, proud to say) they have never read any book on the topic.

Equally there appear to be hundreds of courses, from half-day "cheap and cheerful" to awesomely expensive three-week courses at top business schools. Through case-studies and lectures, games and videos, one supposedly acquires those magic properties, insights or values that lead to superior leadership.

Again it is more surprising how few leaders, good and great, big and small, competent or incompetent, have ever been on one of these courses. Many look upon them with cynical amusement.

How then does one learn "how to become a leader?" Primarily by being led. Ask any 50-year-old who most influenced them as a business leader and they usually nominate a person who led them 20 or 30 years before.

Trainers find it easy and helpful to get people to do the "good boss/bad boss" comparison. They want to generate the differentiating characteristics that clearly discriminated. It's not hard to imagine the list. Good bosses inspire; they give clear directions; set achievable goals; provide support; put in place helpful adaptive processes and so on.

But it is the little things that people remember. The way agendas were constructed to put the really important stuff at the end. The way the leaders did or did not model the behavior they always talked about.

It often comes as a shock to go into some big organizations that have a history of recruiting young people and developing them. That is they tend to grow their own rather than "buy in" from the outside. Take the police or the National Health Service as examples. Often the skills and training mean this is the best option.

But it does mean that they have strong corporate cultures which may be very resistant to change. The reason is conformity to some often unwritten norms. If you are exposed exclusively to leaders throughout your career who have been inducted and socialized in the same way it is not unnatural to follow their example. There is an accepted and prescribed way to lead. You learn by example.

Thus an organization can have generations of risk-averse leaders; generations of those who under- or over delegate; generations of bullies or softies. They replicate management style. That is precisely why governments favor bringing in success-proven private sector leaders to "shake up" sleepy public sector institutions. They are there to challenge assumptions, to question why things are done this way.

Many people will admit to both their delight and their concern at being nominated a leader for the first time. They like all the perks but fear the responsibilities. Some phone up old pals for a spot of advice. What precisely does this leadership lark involve? A few sage do's and don'ts can help. But most replicate what they personally have experienced.

So is it fair to punish incompetent leaders who have only experienced incompetent leadership? Is it equally unfair to lionize those who excel because they were given excellent examples?

If you lead as you were led, it behoves selectors to inquire more closely about a person's job history and about their good and bad role-models.

Higher-educational psychiatric disorders

The academic life is still portrayed as civilized, gentle, and privileged in much of the media. This, despite report after report of academic stress and breakdown as research-trained and selected dons are forced to embrace change from students evaluating them more than they ever did, as well as the new prospect of having to screen candidates for the educational background of their parents. Many are now falling to a whole range of newly discovered academic maladies.

Higher education has certainly changed dramatically in the last fifty years. There are now three times as many universities as there were in 1945. They seem to come and go, rebrand and relabel with great aplomb. What happened to London Guildhall or the University of Luton?

There are now dozens of professors. There are *ad hominem* and titular, regius and emeritus, visiting and special. Everyone, it seems, is a professor these days.

And worse, there are research assessment and teaching assessment exercises and reports. Nosey outsiders come in to do quality audits. In the old days it was a cozy affair, where the head of department – the only professor – would phone an old pal from his Oxford or Cambridge college, who would enjoy a few early June days in a provincial city casting a wise eye over the exams. No longer.

It is no wonder there is now talk of stress among lecturers. Read some reports and they are falling like flies. They line up in droves for early retirement to get away from all the new demands on their time. It is said that it is now difficult to recruit in certain areas.

It seems we need psychiatric help. We need first a good diagnostic system of common ailments and their manifestations. We are in urgent need of a periodic table, a psychiatric DSM (Diagnostic and Statistical Manual-V) system that begins to classify those ever increasing maladies. The following offers a first go:

1. Sociopathic *admissions* complex – A persistent worry that one's admissions policies and procedures are failing, which is causing all

those bright, hard-working, well-heeled students to go to one's great competitors.

2. Defensive *assignment* syndrome – The dread of marking assignments where if you don't give demanding and now litigious students all a starred first they will cause mayhem.

3. Bi-polar *ethics committee* obsession – Rapid changes from loving to loathing these committees, depending on whether they are blocking others' or your own research activity.

4. Defensive *examination* dysfunction – The terrible worry that one really is dumbing down either the exam questions or simply being far too lenient in the marking, accounting for the inexorable and mysterious rise in firsts, year-on-year.

5. Ideational *external examiner* impulse – The Aspergers-like inclination to admit publicly that the external examiner is an ex-lover of the head of department and a mere token.

6. Degenerative *grant income* neurosis – The persistent, consistent and insistent knowledge that grant size is the only thing the vice-chancellor really thinks about – and that one's own is too meager.

7. Adolescent *lecture* inhibition – The overwhelming desire to offload as many lectures as possible onto naïve new colleagues. It may also be accompanied by trying to develop a very complex and obscure course that gets canceled because no students are interested.

8. Bygone-era *nostalgia* syndrome. That terrible and frequent yearning for chalk and overhead projectors in a lecture theatre where the felt-tipped pens have all run out (or don't work on whiteboards) and the PowerPoint presentation setup is beyond one's understanding.

9. Hysterical *promotion* symptoms – A chronic complaint that hits the 50-year-old senior lecturer academic who worries incessantly (and continuously) about ever moving up to that magical full-professorial status and the marginally improved pension that it means.

10. Post-traumatic *publication* fetish – This is a low-self-esteem disorder about size and quality. It is manifest in various ways: cynical attacks on the unscholarliness of the "publish and perish" brigade; clever ways to make conference posters look like publications on one's CV; having many references to profound-sounding books and papers as "in preparation."

11. Suicidal *research* deficit – A personality disorder related to paranoia that leads one to believe one's research output is too modest, too feeble,

or more obviously too little to avoid being offered early retirement. It is frequently a co-morbid disorder with the one above.

12. Unconscious *peer-review* withdrawal – The knowledge that peer review means little more than bitchy, petty, anonymous remarks on years of work. The only way to stop the nastiness is to stop writing, which of course leads to the previous syndrome.

13. Borderline *restructuring* psychosis – A disassociative state induced by pension-related desire to embrace continuous management-driven change to effective practices, combined with the unspeakable suspicion that tried-and-tested methods have some merit.

14. Psychosexual *sabbatical* fixation – The dreamlike state of fantasizing about a year swanning about on a rich American campus in the sunshine interacting with young minds and producing your *magnum opus*.

15. Undifferentiated *seminar* disturbance – The illusion that most seminars are Quaker Meetings but where "the spirit" appears to move no one to speak at all. It represents a major problem to many and appears to have no cure.

16. Substance-fueled *student assessment* breakdown – Claret- or Chardonnay-induced outbursts in essay marking where the anxiety and boredom lead to periodic shrieking, weeping or hysterical laughter. The worry is that somehow you are personally to blame for this incredible display of ignorance.

17. Abnormal *supervision* reaction – The sudden realization that supervising rich, full-fee-paying, foreign students is a terrifying, locked-in process somewhere between counseling and full psychoanalysis where you are trapped for years and years, ending with writing the whole darn thesis yourself.

18. Chronic *(moral)* tutor malady – The real worry that you are not sure exactly what a moral tutor is or should be doing; and whether it has anything to do with morals at all.

19. Lecturer's malignant progressive *somnambulismphobia* – The ever more frequent recurrence of a nightmare that you are pacing up and down trying to give a lecture without notes on a topic you know little about, only to find on waking that you are indeed doing that in your pajamas.

20. Deluded psychiatrist's *narcissistic* obsession – The curious belief that listing all the above and even more peculiar syndromes are furthering science, your career or indeed the welfare of your colleagues.

Hurrah for managerialism

There is a new "ism" around. And like most isms it has a rather negative connotation, though the ideas have been around for ages. It's called managerialism. It is said with a sneer, mainly by those who have always been against the very notion of management.

What are the basic characteristics of managerialism?

- *Performance rather than service management* – The old private vs. public sector divide where the former set and measured performance goals while the latter used service in the loyalty rather than the customer-based sense. It's about the idea of setting performance tasks. Managers focus on performance. You are as good as your last task/accomplishment.
- *Lean and mean* – More with less; efficient use of plant. The central idea is to streamline to ensure that waste in all forms is kept to a minimum. This emphasizes the optimum use of time, money, materials and of course people. Managerialism is about efficiency.
- *Professionalism over amateurism* – The idea is that management is a learnable, professional skill and that all organizations need what Weber described a century ago: a clear chain of command, a feasible span of control. The notion of self-governance by experienced amateurs won't do however clever they may be. Managers need training. Management is a real and important skill.
- *Measurement, monitoring and target-setting* – To know as best as one can how the engine is running and therefore to set up many different mechanisms, from climate surveys to absenteeism logs, to measure individual group, team and organizational performances. The aim is also to set up clear, achievable targets which improve year on year. You cannot manage that which you do not measure.
- *Competition within and between* – This is a very antimonopolistic, free-enterprise ethic which believes that all stakeholders are best served by competition. Survival of the fittest, leanest, meanest. No more subsidizing the ineffectual. No tax on the productive. Shape up or ship out.

- *Outsourcing where appropriate* – The logical consequence of a drive for efficiency and effectiveness is to consider the possibility of outsourcing functions that could prove to be much cheaper and more efficiently delivered. This may involve everything from the canteen to security.
- *Quality control through audit, preferably by outside, disinterested bodies* – This may be voluntary in the sense that an organization puts itself forward to an award-granting body, but more likely all comparable organizations are regularly assessed by trained professionals against an agreed set of standards.
- *The encouragement and acceptance of league tables* – These reveal to all where an organization stands relative to the competition. This means the process is open and competitive.

Many public sector institutions have been "subjected" to managerialism. And with the change has come, of course, massive resistance. From police stations to universities, schools to hospitals the cry has been much the same. There is too much bureaucracy: the effort spent on monitoring has the paradoxical effect of reducing productivity rather than enhancing it. So people have to work harder but achieve less.

Next, because it is the bottom line that drives everything, callous, short-sighted, deeply unempathic decisions are made which backfire in reduced loyalty and respect. All complain about the reduction in their autonomy – that nothing can be done easily, quickly and with volition.

Most of all, complaints are about more pressure to do more in less time with fewer resources. Managers are seen to be remote, duplicitous, with little real understanding of the "business" they are in. In fact, paradoxically, they are not in business and that is the point. They are there to provide a public service.

These managers also pay themselves outrageous salaries, give themselves fancy titles and many perks. Some even get medals from a grateful government.

So it's all doom and gloom then? It's 1984. The manager is Big Brother. So managerialism is all part of the capitalist, globalizing, dehumanization of the workplace.

The question, of course, for the anti-managerialist is, what is the alternative? Some have rather short memories of dealing with organizations that rejoiced in their autonomy; that did things their way, in their good time; to the standards they set.

The opponents of managerialism look back to a non-existent time when benevolent, humanitarian amateurs ran multi-million-pound organizations and everyone was happy. Staff perhaps; customers and shareholders rarely.

There are certainly valid criticisms of the excesses of zealous managerialism. But it is too easy to snipe at those whose task it is to help make organizations survive and thrive.

Identity at work

Hand out some personality-type questionnaires to a group of middle or senior managers. Explain all that stuff about "no right or wrong answers," "no time constraints," "just asking you to specify your preferences and typical behaviors." And then the question *always* asked by a woman, *never* a man: "Shall I respond as I am at home or as I am at work?"

Aha – the split personality? I the mother vs. I the manager? Personal identity vs. shared identity.

Certainly organizations want you to identify with them. They want you to be proud to flash the card, wear the uniform, drop the name. You are, for some people, what you do. Your job title, your company, your product or service defines you. For good or ill. Hence some try to hide their work identity while others rejoice in it, finding it hard to let it go on retirement.

Indeed some people show pathological over-identification with their organization. They are who they work for. Perhaps the organization in some way fills a void, replaces some inner emptiness, gives a coherent, positive sense of self. Organizations can be addictive in the sense that people cannot let them go. Witness the way retired men cling onto titles from long-jettisoned organizations, even though the question remains of who got rid of whom (and why).

But over-identification might be a curse. The over-identified might be vulnerable to breaking laws and rules to benefit their organization. Groups of them might suffer from group-think and all have identical ideas about how to protect or further the organization.

Of course, the opposite can also occur. Here the individuals see themselves as having very different attributes from the organization. This disconnection often enhances their sense of uniqueness and separateness and leads to evaluating the organization negatively. This is usually manifest in terms of a perceived difference in values.

It is unlikely that those experiencing organizational dis-identification joined the company in that state. Their disenchantment, distancing and dis-identification often occurs after organizational change, a breach of psychological contract, a gradual distrust of the organizational ideology or a decline in the reputation of the company.

So people hide the fact of where they work. This can be quite a taxing activity. They also bad-mouth the organization. They feel misfits and behave accordingly.

And then there are those with incongruent multiple identities. You can see this at middle-class parties, weddings or other occasions where individuals bring together family and friends from very different parts of their lives. It's as if people have shown part of themselves to different groups. A young man can be "the wild boy-racer," "the aspiring entrepreneur," "the sensitive musician" and "the caring father" at the same time. People segment themselves, never quite able or willing to integrate those segments. Hence the work self and the home self.

For some the multiple-identity approach can be really healthy and adaptive. But for others the energy devoted to keeping the selves apart and the sense of self-fragmentation is just too psychologically costly.

And then of course there are the ambivalent identities. Ambivalence means alternating. It is usually a reaction to conflict. Thus what if you are a higher-flyer in a greedy organization? What if the job provides you with wonderful developmental experiences but takes you away from important parental duties? Answer – you waver. This makes you unpredictable. And it can be tiring living with the conflict all the time.

So how to help people come to a healthy understanding of who they are within the organization and preventing over-, under-, multiple or ambivalent identification?

This can be very important for people in "dirty" jobs that have stigma and "taint," or those with very high demands on their identity. Think priests and prostitutes; tobacco workers and tax inspectors; sewer maintenance engineers and realtors.

Such people can be helped to separate role from identity, to set limits and to find a higher-order identity. They can be encouraged to flip an on–off switch. Equally, those who experience dis-identification may be encouraged to merge the role with their personal identity, to infuse the self into the task.

Some merely require an adjustment in their need for identification, while others may need a re-energizing of their non-work life in order to enable their identity to come from that. Sociologists now talk of the "third place" for identity acquisition. First the home, then work. Third, community, leisure, social, religious groups. They can offer a lot in terms of helping people know who they are.

So try the old sentence completion test. Complete the following sentence "I am . . . " twenty times. You might be surprised about who you think you are!

Intelligence and wealth

Studies from America and Britain have shown a clear link between height and income. Taller people get paid more.

The data are pretty robust, but the explanations are highly contested. Is it that height is related to class, good feeding and good education? Or is it that tall people are simply more confident, which is a good predictor of success even if only modestly related to ability?

It has been demonstrated that the same is true of good looks. Handsome actors get more parts; good-looking politicians are elected more often; attractive directors become the CEO. Sure there are many exceptions: short, bald, turnip-faced people at the top. But is the idea not generally true? Survival of the prettiest. The good-looking shall inherit the earth.

If appearance is (unfairly) related to wealth, what about ability? Surely the more able do better educationally and therefore get better jobs, which are better paid? But do you have to be bright to be rich? There appear to be other factors as well.

The data now exist to answer some of these questions. An American economist (Zagorsky 2007) has reported results from a detailed longitudinal study of thousands of baby boomers born between 1957 and 1964. They have been interviewed and tested over 20 times in their 40 or 50 years, so a great quantity of data are available on them. In this study the author looked at four factors:

- *IQ test scores* – They all sat a ten-test battery, with tests of everything from general science through arithmetic, reasoning and word knowledge to paragraph comprehension. These were sat in 1980.
- *Income* – This was calculated in 2004 and included data on pre-tax income from wages, salaries, tips and self-employment, plus welfare payments, child support, alimony and gifts.
- *Wealth* – This was a careful calculation of net worth based on assets and liabilities: market value of home, mortgages, savings, possessions, stocks and bonds.
- *Financial distress* – This was simply defined as living beyond one's means, and measured three things: amount owed on credit cards; a history of missing out on payments; evidence of bankruptcy.

Of course, other factors were taken into account like their ethnic origins, education, marital status, whether they smoked, as well as personality factors, their self-esteem and how much they feel in control of their life.

The results were pretty impressive, showing a nearly linear pattern. Those with IQs of 75 or below had a net worth of less than £3,000 while those with the average score of 100 had nearly £30,000 and those with 125 and above around twice that at £65,000.

Looking at the simple correlation evidence the following was clear. Those with higher IQ scores were better educated and had higher incomes. They also had higher self-esteem and a greater sense of personal control and mastery over their lives.

However the researcher also did the sexy stats: (various) types of regression analysis to look at the power of IQ to predict financial variables while taking into account the other factors involved.

And the results? Yes (unexpectedly) intelligence does predict income. Each single point increase in IQ is associated with £100 to £300 per year. Put another way the difference between the annual income of a really bright person (IQ over 130, in the top 2 per cent) compared with the average person (IQ at 100) is between £3,000 and £9,000.

But the results do not stack up for wealth. Age, ethnic and personality variables seemed more important. There was also no linear relationship between IQ and financial distress although the trend was clear and significant. Thus around 12 per cent of IQ 80 had credit card debt, while it was 6 per cent for those with IQ over 125. Equally 25 per cent of those at the bottom missed payments compared to 12 per cent at the top of the IQ range.

So the author concludes that being bright does not convey any particular advantage on two of the three key dimensions of financial success. He suggests that there are possible psychological factors that more powerfully drive material wealth accumulation. Those include desire for immediate or deferred satisfaction, tolerance or intolerance for taking risks, and susceptibility to social influence.

And of course there is luck and the opportunistic desire to exploit it. As Getty said, the three secrets of getting rich are: Get up Early; Work Hard; Strike Oil.

The author of this study seems to be very sensitive to the American Dream ideology where anybody can become rich or president or whatever. He writes, "[I]ndividuals with low intelligence should not believe they are handicapped in achieving financial success, nor should high intelligence people believe they have an advantage." Hmmm – not sure on this. Maybe there is a path from intelligence through education and self-belief to wealth.

To misquote a woman who married thrice into wealth, "You can never be too bright or too rich," and the two are indeed (modestly) related.

Reference

Zagorsky, J. L. (2007) "Do You Have to Be Smart to Be Rich? The Impact of IQ on Wealth, Income and Financial Distress," *Intelligence*, 35, 489–501.

Leadership as a demotivator

Most people know the work of three psychologists: Freud, who was all about sex, Maslow, who built a pyramidal hierarchy of needs, and Herzberg, who said money was a hygiene factor.

It's fifty years since Herzberg and colleagues published their first book on job attitudes and motivation. In a review of the current literature they found no systematic or replicable relationship between job attitudes and work performance. They concluded that researchers of the time had never distinguished between job satisfaction and job dissatisfaction. Their unique contribution was that although we think of job satisfaction as a continuum from high to low, good to bad, the two ends are determined by very different factors.

That is, some things prevent satisfaction – they are called hygiene factors or dissatisfiers – while others (quite different) cause (encourage, lead to, facilitate) job satisfaction and are called motivational factors or satisfiers.

Most managers "remember" three things about the theory. Paradoxically money is a hygiene factor; its primary power is to demotivate if people are not paid fairly, not paid according to market forces, not paid according to their input. Second, they recall that motivation is all about personal achievement, growth and recognition. Third, they recall it means that jobs have to be enriched because people respond best when engaged.

Actually the academics gave up on Herzberg years ago. They found little evidence for his theory. The various factors never fell into the two groups neatly; some from both groups could have the opposite effect specified by the theory; and there are large differences in people's responses in the job.

The whole job satisfaction issue never goes away, but merely gets repackaged. So "satisfaction" became "commitment" and then "engagement." There are now huge consultancies based on measuring morale; on plotting the pulse of the people in the organization. The idea is still that motivation, or engagement, or satisfaction is directly linked to performance. Maybe. But it is (alas) more complicated than that.

Curiously most trainers and reviewers have overlooked, forgotten, or ignored one of Herzberg's more interesting and crucial findings. Leadership (he called it supervision) was a hygiene factor; only a possible demotivator. Your relationship with your boss had much greater power to demotivate than motivate.

This is not what the leadership industry wants to hear. Millions are spent head-hunting, coaching and training for leadership. We are told fanciful and improbable stories of brilliant, brave and bold leaders saving companies or taking them to new heights. Shareholders, indeed all stakeholders, pray for these mystical creatures to save the day, encourage growth and go ever upwards and onwards.

But if Herzberg is right then individual and business unit performance is not dependent on charm, charisma or conscientiousness. There is plenty of evidence to support the "leadership can only demotivate" theory. Try conducting job exit interviews. It is true that people leave their bosses, not their organizations. Look at job analysis and see how much time and effort is spent avoiding supervisor input. And given the amount of pathology and incompetence around in senior management, if leadership were that important then many companies would fail.

What is important is business unit performance however measured and assessed. The question therefore is one of team effectiveness. What factors contribute most to the productivity of individuals and teams? The simple causal view is that leaders affect morale, which affects performance. Very simple? No, very simple-minded.

But also it ignores the data. Staff morale *is* related to leadership style, but modestly. An individual's personality is consistently a better predictor of morale. There are carriers of gloom, negativity and dissatisfaction and there are uplifting, positive, enthusiastic types. Leadership has little impact on disposition.

And of course there are adaptive, efficient and flexible work processes, workable and appropriate technology and marketing.

Leadership is quite simply lower on the list of factors that lead to success. But it is surprisingly powerful in its ability to alienate. This is the Herzbergian implication. Bad leaders demotivate. Good leaders don't improve morale and performance – they just don't impede it.

And the implication of all this? It's about select out, not select in. It's about identifying and removing bad leaders. Incompetent, uninspiring, cold bosses can create mayhem in a very short period of time. Notice how, in a bar or restaurant, the fact that it's "under new management" can create chaos in weeks. Good staff leave in droves.

So was old Herzberg right then? Probably it's a bit of an oversimplification. But a much-needed correction to all that heroic CEO leadership nonsense. It seems experientially true. The power and speed of the impact of bad supervisors and leaders on business performance is always greater than that of good ones.

Leadership potential

Every organization understands that it needs to recruit and retain talented leaders for the future. As a result there has been a *"war for talent"* as organizations search top universities, business schools and indeed their competitors for young people with potential.

A central question in this quest is to know what one is looking for, and secondly how to assess or measure it. There is a research literature on this topic, covered below, but to be most useful, line-managers need a jargon-free and accessible toolkit which explains *what to look for* and *how to measure it*.

Over the past fifty years there has been a sustained effort to find the individual difference factors which characterize the successful business leader. Dozens of studies in the management and social sciences have yielded similar results. That is, researchers looking at leadership in different countries, in different business sectors, and at different stages in the business cycle have consistently shown up the *same set of factors*. It is therefore these characteristics that one needs to search out to be sure people have the sort of leadership potential one is after.

Five factors come up again and again. Most are relatively easy to specify and measure by a variety of standard techniques like structured job interview, references, job history; but also, importantly, psychometric tests measuring both ability (intelligence) and preferences (personality).

The five factors and how to measure them:

1. Cognitive ability

The single best predictor of leadership/management success is intelligence, particularly at higher levels of management. This is not to be confused with formal education, though they are modestly related. Managers need to be *bright enough*: that is they require some minimum level of intelligence to do the job well. As one goes up the organization, jobs become more complex: one needs to be more intelligent to do them well. Further things can change or need changing and leaders have to understand those issues.

The research literature indicates a number of important points with respect to intelligence:

- Followers like, respect and support brighter leaders.
- Brighter leaders are both seen as, and are, more effective than less-bright leaders.
- Brighter leaders are better at transforming organizations and managing change.
- Brighter leaders have more (intellectual) self-confidence and suffer less stress.
- Brighter leaders learn faster, are more positive about personal growth and are more adaptable.

All senior management positions require a basic level of intelligence which can be specified as a cutoff score on tests. This is not to say that leaders need to be exceptionally able; however, it is important they reach a minimum level.

The measurement of intelligence is both straightforward and accurate. There are numerous tests to choose from which all yield similar results. Many have been designed to test thinking and reasoning in business con-texts. It is advisable to use two or three shorter tests so as to avoid bias or error. Testing need not take more than *half an hour*.

It is very important to choose tests that do not disadvantage any groups such as those for whom English is not their first language, dyslexic indi-viduals and so on. This area is well researched and appropriate tests may easily be sought.

2. Stability

Senior management and leadership positions always involve stress. People have to make hard decisions, take risks, face criticism and endure setbacks. They need to be hardy and resilient to respond to the pace and challenges of modern business life.

The single best predictor of stress reactions is a person's emotional stability. Less stable people are, in essence, prone to neuroses. Unstable people tend to be tense, touchy and thin-skinned. They can have rapidly fluctuating moods, and be very brittle.

The research literature suggests that:

- Unstable people are prone to anxiety and depression. They often make bad decisions because of this.

- Unstable people are particularly vulnerable to stress and stress-related illness. Neurosis is closely related to absenteeism.
- Unstable people can be self-pitying, self-defeating and prone to a depressive, gloomy outlook.
- Followers report having considerable difficulty with the moodiness and vulnerability of unstable managers.
- Stable leaders, by contrast, cope well under inevitable periods of stress.
- Stable leaders tend to have healthy, adaptable coping strategies whereas the opposite is true for their less able colleagues.

Stability is relatively easy to measure through questionnaires, as well as by looking at an individual's health record. It can also be subtly assessed via references. While it is true that people tend to under-report their anxiety, vulnerability and self-consciousness on questionnaires, there is ample evidence that these measures are reliable and valid and can pick up signs of stability and instability.

3. Conscientiousness

Every business leader needs to be hardworking and self-disciplined. Business leaders have to be dependable, reliable and responsible. They need to be responsive to various stakeholders – their staff, colleagues, customers and shareholders. They have to learn to be efficient and organized. They need to understand the need to plan ahead and to ensure things are always done to the required standard.

The research literature has shown the following:

- Conscientiousness is closely related to competence, which is one of the highest-rated virtues followers want in their managers.
- Conscientiousness determines a manager's dedication, deliberation and dutifulness.
- Conscientious leaders are hard-working but they learn to work "smart" as well as long hours. They understand when and why they need to go the extra mile.
- Conscientious leaders tend to be achievement-oriented and aspirational for themselves and others.
- Conscientious leaders deliver on their promises, which are realistic, and they tend to follow ethical rules sensibly and sensitively.

Conscientiousness, the work ethic or prudence is measured straightforwardly by questionnaire and through the examination of a person's track record. People are very quickly observed by others to be well-organized and constantly striving to reach their goals. On the other hand the easygoing, poorly organized, often careless and rarely planful individual is not difficult to spot. These observable behaviors come through on references and 360-degree feedback reports.

4. Emotional intelligence

Management and leadership is a social activity. Leaders have to inspire and support their staff. They are in the motivation business. They have to understand themselves and other people. Emotional intelligence, in essence, involves understanding and being able to influence other people. But it also involves self-understanding or awareness and the knowledge of how to deal with setbacks. Emotional intelligence is essentially about having social skills, charm and insight. Emotionally intelligent leaders understand the importance and power of emotions in everyday life. They are good at the emotional regulation of everyday life.

The research literature shows that:

- Emotionally intelligent leaders are liked, trusted and admired most by their staff.
- Leaders with high EQ always get the best out of their staff and are hence highly productive.
- High-EQ leaders are particularly successful in difficult times when organizations are under considerable pressure.
- High-EQ leaders understand the important psychological needs of their key staff members and are very good at getting the best out of them.
- Emotional intelligence is linked to being more assertive, empathic, optimistic and self-motivated.

There are many tests of emotional intelligence but only a few that have been researched well. Once again, interviewers and references help in finding out about emotional intelligence once people know what things to look for. Questionnaire measures tend to provide a very good all-round picture of the emotional self-awareness and skills of managers.

5. Motivation

Motivation is the engine of leadership success but it needs direction. People are quite clearly motivated by different things – power, influence, control, recognition. The great problem with the concept of motivation is that it appears at the same time both all-encompassing *and* vague. People are motivated to achieve a goal: the more motivated they are the more time, effort and energy they are willing to put into achieving that goal. More importantly most of these goals are not easily satisfied and this motivation does not stop once they have been achieved. This is true of both psychological goals like recognition and more objective goals like monetary reward.

The research literature suggests the following:

- All people are motivated to seek recognition and reward from those they work for, to boost their self-esteem.
- Motivated leaders are often particularly sensitive to issues around fairness – that is that reward is directly related to effort, that output and input are closely linked.
- Motivated leaders have realistic expectations and set for themselves and others attainable but stretched goals.
- Motivated leaders understand the importance of giving and receiving feedback.
- Motivated leaders are less distracted by setbacks.

Motivated leaders learn from their mistakes and direct their efforts most efficiently.

Of all the five factors motivation is often most difficult to measure. This is primarily because people cannot, rather than will not, always tell you what really motivates them. Clearly some people seek out different rewards than others. But all are motivated by recognition and by personal achievement. There are questionnaires that measure a person's values or goals which help explain what they are specifically motivated to achieve. However, interview references and track record give good details about a person's energy, hunger or drive. This explains therefore both what specifically motivates people and how much energy they put into the task.

Conclusion

There are five definable, measurable and necessary characteristics of highly successful leaders. They need to be bright, stable, hardworking and socially skilled, and possess drive. These characteristics are necessary but possibly not sufficient in the sense that someone may need others as well.

It is important to define the behaviors associated with their characteristics so that non-specialist line managers are clear about what they are looking for and why. Further it is always important to inspect the total profile of an individual. There will of course be important differences between successful leaders. Yet it is crucial that they all have the above characteristics to thrive and prosper in a changing, complex and challenging business environment.

Lookism at work

How many types of discrimination can you list? Race, religion, disability? And age discrimination, of course. All four of these are illegal in the sense that it is against the law to use these primarily (indeed at all) as criteria for accepting or rejecting job candidates.

It is a funny word, discrimination. It used to be a virtue. Magazines of the 1950s show "chaps with hats" choosing, nay "insisting on," a particular brand of product because they were "people of taste and discrimination." You could tell the difference; perceive subtle but important features; choose the better one.

But discrimination became a bad word and differentiation a good one. And then we had positive discrimination, which meant that, unless you put the "p" word in front, all discrimination was negative, evil, immoral and so on.

Age discrimination is the latest to be subject to legislation. Old application forms have to be redrafted to drop the "date of birth" box. CVs now contain many kinds of intimate self-disclosure such as "personal values" and "passions" – but omit age. It's usually not that difficult to work out a candidate's age from dates of matriculation, graduation and so on. So now some CVs drop all dates and nervous HR people don't inquire.

And the application process has, for most people, dropped the habit of asking for a recent photograph. This was mainly for the purpose of identification. Imposters have been known to take tests for other people. And photographs can help accurately jog the memory of interviewers who might see as many as a dozen candidates in a row.

Interviewers who remember the photograph requirement might recall that some photographs were clearly much more flattering than others. Some candidates were almost unrecognizable from their photos. An interesting fact for the interviewer: did it give clues to impression management (effectively telling lies about yourself) or self-delusion (effectively believing your own propaganda)? Was it particularly useful in service jobs?

Photographs are a no-no now because of a new discrimination: *lookism.* This has close cousins of heightism and weightism which could be called *shapism.* The lookists/shapists argue that people do better at work (are selected, promoted, rewarded) on their looks more than performance, which is unfair. Survival of the prettiest! The beautiful shall inherit the earth.

Unfortunately there is abundant research evidence to prove that this is true. Overweight people (as shown in photographs) are less likely to be selected for interviews and, if they make that stage, less likely to get the job. Very short people, particularly men, don't fare too well. The bald and bearded, those with thick lenses, or poor skin, or uneven teeth, are all handicapped. What is beautiful is good. Attractive people spend less time in mental hospitals, receive smaller/lower fines and prison sentences and are more likely to be elected leaders.

And clearly looks are important in some jobs more than others. Lookism seems rampant in the performing arts. And possibly in many service jobs.

There are three problems with the issue of the psychology of attractiveness, the issue of lookism and issues of discrimination. The *first* is the problem of subjectivity. There is often considerable agreement about the very beautiful and very ugly, but much less consensus about those in between. There are websites, support groups and fan clubs of people with very particular characteristics. Some individuals find plump voluptuousness attractive. Beauty, indeed attractiveness, like contact lenses might be almost entirely in the eye of the beholder. This makes discrimination legislation or even guidelines very problematic.

But the *second* issue is much hotter. It has been suggested that looks are related to job performance: attractive people do out-perform their less attractive colleagues! How? There are various mechanisms suggested to account for this. On the simplest social learning theory level, attractive people are more self-confident as a result of the way they have been treated in the past. They have been privileged, favored and rewarded. Evolutionary psychologists have proposed the unthinkable and suggested there are good reasons to believe attractiveness is linked with intelligence, which is itself a good predictor of job success.

More obviously, the public respond well to more attractive people. Better-looking people are more persuasive. They sell more, get more tips, are more liked. Unfair perhaps – but then life is unfair.

Third, some activities require a certain shape. People might need a certain strength, agility, stretch and so on. They might need 20/20 vision. Have all these issues have been considered in the disability legislation?

There might be downsides to being good-looking with an ideal shape. People with good looks can be arrogant, narcissistic, spoilt: think supermodels, teenage actresses. They can be lazy, relying on their looks rather than their skills, perseverance or simply hard work. And they may be very low on empathy and insight because they have not had to learn these skills.

Heightism, lookism and weightism are soon to be on the agenda of the "discrimination at work" enthusiasts. They are certainly right to point out that attractiveness does affect every aspect of our lives, and our success at work. But the real issue is how best to deal with that fact.

Management neurosis

Psychiatrists now recognize a dozen or so personality disorders which fit nicely into the three-fold scheme. And, more recently, psychologists who study behavior at work have noted how useful this system is in describing management failure.

Those who move towards others can be agreeable, sociable, and dutiful. But their fault is deferring to tyrants, being too easily intimated and not "kicking ass" when it is required. Often they won't be sufficiently assertive in clarifying their own and their staff's actual and real needs, which can easily result in burnout.

Others try too hard to please by being super-diligent and imposing unrealistically high standards on themselves and others. This can lead to micromanagement, inability to delegate and the disempowerment of others.

Moving towards others can be adaptive and healthy. It results in failure when friendship turns to dependence; when desire to please turns to perfectionism; when looking and moving towards (powerful) others leads to neglecting junior staff or driving them to distraction.

Habitually moving away from others too has its problems. The skeptical, cautious and reserved manager can create serious issues. Skepticism is certainly better than cynicism, but it is marked by a distrust of all others including superiors, peers and subordinates. These managers doubt everyone's motives. They may question others' integrity and make them feel distinctly uneasy and unaccepted.

The cautious can't make up their minds. Their fear of error paralyses them. Of course they resist change, sticking out for "tried and tested" solutions which may alas be no longer relevant. Their staff become frustrated because they are not clearly directed. And they can be punished for the slightest error.

Some who move away from others fail as a result of their excitability, mood swings and emotional outbursts. They seem unable to sustain anything: projects, relationships, goals. Finally there are those who move away from others in order to pursue with their own agenda. Their self-obsession means they don't manage their staff well, neither setting expectations and then following team commitments through, nor doing the simple essentials of management.

And then there are those who move against others. Again, they come in various disguises and all are undesirable. First there are the fearless, the bold and the risk-takers. They take charge with feelings of personal destiny and entitlement. But if things go wrong – as they surely do – they are quick to unload total blame onto others. Despite their swashbuckling confidence and a willingness to "take anybody on," they fail desperately to learn from experience and one cocked-up grand plan follows another.

More dangerous and often more successful for longer periods are the deceiving, rule-breaking, mischievous leaders. They break the rules (and the law), ignoring commitments, promises and contracts. They talk their way out of all problems and seem completely amoral. They work against everyone and everything, seeking only to serve their own rules.

Lastly there are the imaginative, eccentric "genius" types who can make very odd decisions and show some strange behaviors. Others move away from them as actively as they move away from others.

We all feel anxious at times: insecure, inadequate, self-doubting. The psychoanalysts showed how people try to deal with these facts of life. But it has been the work psychologists who have shown how these play out in business to the detriment of all stakeholders.

Modern management styles

What happened to MBWA (management by walking around) or the "one-minute manager"? Perhaps the managers who spent all their time walking around lost their way, forgot to do some planning or did not notice the need for marketing.

And who has quality circles now? Who dresses down on Friday? Why no more process re-engineering or managers called coaches? Their demise may be a source of fun to outsiders who observe them – though perhaps less amusing to those at the sharp end of silver-bullet, magic-potion management.

Individual managers will always do their own thing, no matter what happens to management fads. A heady mixture of personality, preferences and pathology means that individual managers often adopt quirky styles they believe to be effective. In minor doses these are little more than amusing quirks. Taken to extreme they can lead to disaster.

- *Acronym management* – This is in-group-abbreviation management. "Has the CFO completed his KRAs for the FRM?" The aim is to speak a private language that excludes all non-speakers. The more you can speak the jargon, the closer you are to the center of power.
- *Amnesic management* – This is management by forgetting, but highly selective forgetting, for example the intensity of disagreements at meetings, or, more seriously but most of all, serious promises made to others. Alzheimer's management is a more extreme version.
- *Anecdotal management* – This is story-telling, ripping-yarn, guru-parable management. Direction is given and decisions made by use of curiously repeated anecdotes of long-past events that often have seemingly nothing to do with the problems in hand.
- *Blue-sky management* – This is theoretical, futurological, big-picture management. It is not about the grubby here-and-now, nor the tedium of appraisals, balance sheets or customer satisfaction. It is the magic world of business gurus. Managers believe their job is to understand the big issues and all else will follow.
- *Corporate entertaining management* – Not only is the customer king but he or she frequently needs a good lunch and a memorably sponsored

event. The marketing budget is spent with enthusiasm by this party-going manager who loves to be at the center of things.

- *Doppler-effect management* – This is achieved by walking very fast and purposefully in public places. Conversations are all soundbites about future meetings – "We must link up!" or "Lunch soon!" These are said earnestly just before disappearing upstairs, down in an elevator or round the corner.

- *E-mail management* – This is non-contact management by sending continual chevron urgent missives, instructions, minutes and memos. It is measured by the word, not by the impact. Curiously, follow-up on any of the bewildering babble to emerge from the fingertips of these shy managers seems unimportant.

- *PA management* – This is management by having a bossy secretary do all the (dirty) work. She (for it always is) is usually a mixture of Attila the Hun and Carry On Matron. Often the PA is the power behind the throne.

- *Personal development management* – This is management by degrees; by studying; by the organization paying for the manager to complete a very expensive MBA. Managers are frequently on courses, completing assignments or on fact-finding missions. Good for their career, bad for the business.

- *Peer meeting management* – This is management by talking to other managers in and outside the business – literally. This is supposed to reduce the silo problem, ensure better integration and improve communication. Equally, meeting managers from other similar businesses (size, sector) in nice hotels in the (ideally foreign) country is even better for gossip and a free lunch.

- *Reorganization management* – This is organogram, cage-rattling management that involves fiddling with the structure of the organization. This is the amateur version of process re-engineering. Just as people get used to the new structure and system, they are reorganized.

- *Secrecy management* – This is hush-hush style management. Information is power so it needs to be kept out of the hands of practically everyone. The secret of secrecy management is being "in the know" and, more important, making sure nobody else is.

- *Spiritual management* – These are the David Icke-type managers who may manifest their style with crystals on their desk or strange pictures on the wall. This is management by shared beliefs; not so much supernatural people as supernatural powers. Believing leads to the release of (mysterious) energy, synergy, ideas and the like.

- *Total obedience management* – this is your no-nonsense, sergeant-major, oldfashioned Gradgrind approach. A manager's job is to give orders, the staff's is to obey: Amen. All this consultative, democratic, first-among-equals stuff is sheer piffle. Manager knows best; tells you what to do; you do it.

Moving toward, against and away from others

Funny how many things come in threes. Over the years writers, clinicians and personality theorists have attempted to map the very basic dimensions of human personality. Naturally there have been arguments, disputes and fights over the number and labeling of the factors.

The fights have been as much about eponymous fame as theory and data. People squabble over labels. Are people neurotic, or high in negative affectivity? Some talked of low adjustment or anxiety-proneness. Some loved splitting simple factors in two and then in two again.

Go the web if you want to see the result of all this taxonomic effort. Despite the scientists calling for parsimony and even agreeing on a restricted number of fundamental traits, the marketplace has called for more. People really don't like the idea of their rich, multifactored personality being reduced to three or five (simple) numbers.

But there is an elegant simplicity in parsimony. One taxonomy was proposed by one of psychoanalysis's few great women. Karen Horney had a pretty consistent background for the early psychoanalytic fraternity. The Hamburg-born daughter of a Danish sea-captain, she studied medicine in Berlin but emigrated to America in the 1930s. She fought with her psychoanalytic friends and mentors, founded her own institute and crafted her own theory. It goes like this (and starts with childhood, of course). To the young child the world is inevitably a frightening, unfriendly and threatening place. The child has to learn strategies to cope with people and circumstances. This occurs by exaggerating one of the three main characteristics of anxiety: helplessness, aggressiveness or detachment. So children learn to move towards people for protection and compliance, against people for domination and mastery or away from people to avoid problems and pain.

These "solutions" are unconscious, compulsive and inflexible, but not mutually exclusive. They become personality dimensions, defense mechanisms and coping strategies. They are at the crux of who we are, how we behave and most particularly how we cope with stress.

- *Moving towards people* – The helpless, weak, child-cum-adult says forgive, love and protect me and don't desert me. I need love and protection. These people become perceptive and caring, but at the cost of repressing their (healthy enough) assertiveness, hostility and selfishness. It is the urge to feel safe that leads to the affection and approval-seeking, but may hide control, exploitative, manipulative and even parasitic tendencies. The potential self-deception leads to feelings of abuse, abandonment and atypical outbursts of rage.

- *Moving against people* – Here the individual becomes safe (and strong) though direct and indirect domination, exploitation, conquest and mastery. People are hostile, hypocritical and deeply untrustworthy. Alas, they believe genuine affection is really non-existent and unattainable. Therefore one needs to be callous, ruthless and inconsiderate – like everybody else. They can, says Horney, often turn into bullies, particularly picking on the weak and helpless because such behaviors are unpleasant reminders of what they really don't like about themselves.

- *Moving away from people* – Here the aim is self-sufficiency. "I am a rock; I am an island," sang Simon and Garfunkel. Such people aim to make no one indispensable or central. The strategy is to numb emotions, overemphasize stoicism and overestimate strength. They back away from emotional attachment. They react strongly to the care and concern of others as being unwarranted, unnecessary and possibly even hostile. Yet, their (deeply) repressed and very natural desire for affiliation and love can cause deep conflict.

Horney's name is now long forgotten but her ideas still attract attention. Indeed many psychologists have noted how her system "fits" with theirs. Thus the famous Hans Eysenck, who also had a three-factor model, saw extraverts as "moving toward" types, neurotics as "moving away" and psychotics as "moving against."

And the psychiatrists too can classify the personality disorders pretty easily. Those moving towards others are likely to be antisocial (mischievous), borderline (excitable), histrionic (colorful) or narcissistic (bold). Those moving away are most likely to be avoidant (cautious), dependent (dutiful) or obsessive-compulsive (diligent). And finally those moving against are possibly likely to be paranoid (skeptical), schizoid (reserved) or schizotypal (imaginative).

All very interesting perhaps, but what has this to do with management, leadership and business issues? The answer is potentially quite a lot. When stressed and frustrated, people react in characteristic ways. Some react by moving towards others requesting help, others against by thrashing out and some by clamming up. These typical reactions may or may not be helpful for those around them. They may send the wrong signal: they may exacerbate the problem; they may alienate supporters.

Knowing the characteristic moves a person makes when anxious can help people predict and understand them. It may be an excellent signaling device. And, if you believe the therapists, it can be changed, though that may take a very long time and be itself painful and expensive.

Negotiation skills courses

Whether they are volunteers or conscripts, people seem to enjoy negotiation skills courses a great deal. They are rated much higher than those other soft-skill courses such as counseling or selecting, presenting or mentoring. The reason seems pretty simple: participants learn and practice a highly transferable skill.

There used to be a joke about the difference between your spouse and a terrorist. Answer: you can negotiate with a terrorist. But how best to do it? There are trained units for this precise task. And of course we have ACAS which, though it does not have the word in its title, is really a negotiation service.

There are, of course, many types of negotiation, from paying a fair price for your carpet in the Grand Bazaar to preventing a damaging and costly strike. You negotiate a price and a pay rise. You negotiate in M&A and management buyouts. Negotiation happens between contractors and suppliers, unions and management, and all the various stakeholders in organizations.

It is not uncommon for a nasty, vicious cycle to develop. Dispute leads to conflict which leads to obstruction. The mud from the bottom of the pool is stirred up. Egos are damaged. Trust is lost. Fear and anger dominate the emotions. Value differences suddenly emerge, implicit expectations are made explicit and don't coincide. And so on. Lawyers are called in.

It is possible to classify both people and organizations as dispute-wise, or skilled or savvy. That is the people are trained and processes are arranged to facilitate negotiation, mediation, arbitration skills. They know how to prevent things escalating, getting out of control and personal.

Some organizations train internal facilitators (or whatever name), others buy in experts. Some believe it benefits the whole organization to put managers on courses to learn some basic skills. The idea is to be sensible, pragmatic, reasonable; to have not legal contracts, but common-sense agreements to problems. To nip them in the bud. To move on to everyone's benefit.

So there are various simple strategies to use. The first is how to *frame the issue*. To move above right and wrong, win or lose, to the big picture where mutual interests are at stake. No-one wins if everybody loses their job. So you might need to move up or down a level in perspective. Down to specific issues where priorities, expectations, values can be easily seen. Best work out where there is agreement. And best also to park some issues that seem too hot, intractable, insurmountable problems. Things change: they may seem less important when other things are rearranged.

Next there is *separating the person and the problem* – the individual and the issue. It's all too easy to do slanderous name-calling; to make wounding personal remarks about another's appearance, approach or values. You need the courtesy and respect stuff found in Parliament (sometimes in court). All that "my learned friend" or "the honorable member for East Cheam." But remember, the issue is not being verbally clever or cryptically sarcastic but solving a problem. Polite, respectful, focused.

Third, there are requirements for *creativity*: for divergent, out-of-the-box thinking. All that "What if?," "Imagine that," axiom-challenging questioning. It shows open-mindedness, an attempt to find a real solution, and can be fun.

And of course there are many opportunities for practicing one's counseling skills. Such as reflecting back, frequent summarizing to show listening, understanding, progress. It's also about being open with discomfort, ambiguity, doubt, assuming that all parties have it.

Exploiting the deeply held *reciprocity norm* is always useful. It is also called matched concessions. I give, you give. And why not surprise them with a small but genuine unilateral concession?

Of course you soon realize that the lines between appraisal, counseling and negotiation skills are very fine. So have some trainers, who use identical exercises for all their people skills. Is not negotiation the selling of one's ideas? Is it not related to healthy assertiveness?

This is what people on negotiation skills courses learn: useful tips and strategies. Naturally there are some specific ideas which don't translate between all courses. Non-directive counseling is not so useful in negotiation, nor is excessive self-disclosure.

But watch a dispute-savvy manager in action. They seem to run a happy ship. Where people are not afraid to air their differences, but where they know they won't get out of control. A useful skill, worth selecting for and developing.

The obsessive-compulsive manager

I am careful; he is perfectionistic; they are obsessional. While psychiatrists and laypeople talk in terms of clinical types, we know all behaviors fall on a continuum from normal and adaptive through to pathological and maladaptive. Often it's the context that defines or categorizes what is normal or not.

So to a group of quality controllers, internal auditors or health and safety people a series of procedures and processes may seem completely sensible, indeed essential. But to the outsider they are ridiculous, time-wasting and expensive.

So what is the obsessive-compulsive manager (OCM)? Where does his condition come from? Can it be cured? Are there subtypes? Certainly one sees various forms of the "pathology:"

- The conscientious OCM: slavishly following and never challenging outdated and petty rules and dim authority figures, mainly through fear of rejection or failure.
- The bureaucratic OCM: these are the rules-and-regulations enforcers who value tradition and identify powerfully with the rule-following ethos, often because they fear the motivational power of their inner impulses.
- The puritanical OCM: those are the punitive, self-righteous, judgmental types whose insistence on strict codes are (often pathetic) attempts, mainly at self-control.
- The parsimonious OCM: those whose legendary meanness and lack of generosity is seen as a defense against loss and others recognizing their inner emptiness.
- The bedeviled OCM: those who feel they have to conform to others' demands against their own wishes, thus experiencing consistent feelings of resentment and conflict.

Overall those working in the field suggest eight characteristic patterns:

1. They appear constrained, serious, tense, with highly regulated appearance and expression. This controls their feelings of insecurity and anger and their abiding fear of disapproval.
2. They always appear formal, correct, deferential – particularly to all those in authority – with a well-articulated sense of morality.
3. They present a slow, rigid, regulated adherence to rules and schedules which can seem somewhere between amusing and pathetic.
4. They appear defensive because they expend a great deal of energy repressing what they believe to be unacceptable images, impulses and thoughts.
5. They manifest a serious discomfort with any negative emotion like defiance, resistance, rebelliousness and resentment in others, but also of course in themselves.
6. They also have a rather odd self-image that rejoices in self-discipline, personal responsibility and a reticence towards levity or any recreational activity.
7. They seem to be able to categorize and compartmentalize parts of their lives, making memories and motives fit nicely into pre-ordained boxes.
8. They are seriously anhedonic, never showing nor approving of pure pleasure.

They psychiatrists say it's a mixture of biological dispositions and temperaments, but also, naturally, life experience. Any experience that chronically threatens self-worth and makes one not trust oneself or feel in control helps bring about the problem. Of course having to follow, uphold, even propagate strict, narrow (and pointless) ethical, moral or religious codes helps the pathological process.

The OCM is not a happy bunny. They wrestle constantly with fear of social disapproval, of losing control and of expressing their hostility to others. And they have a dysfunctional devotion to work and achievement. They try to maintain control through their excessive attention to detail and their anxiety levels go up with all sorts of change, particularly to their carefully honed and preserved social role and persona.

So the OCM doesn't really trust others. They don't delegate, they don't seek help. But their rigidity, orderliness and workaholism can be seen to be advantageous by some. The trouble is "too much of a good thing." They can be prone to burnout and procrastination (till, of course, you do it right).

They don't have good workplace relationships. They frustrate the hell out of their co-workers and therefore do not have the benefits of social support and friendships. As managers their anxiety and mistrust makes them difficult to respect.

So if you have an OCM manager what can you do? You have to perform the whole pretty typical gamut of treatments. Get self-awareness, teach relaxation, bolster self-esteem, teach assertiveness. Helping the OCM get in touch with and express his/her emotions is a really good start. Teaching healthy coping skills is equally important.

Most importantly check that the organizational climate and culture don't actually, explicitly or tacitly approve of, or even call for, obsessive-compulsive behaviours. The long-hours, stress-denying punishment for any minor failure may model O-C behavior. Teamwork, flexibility and a flat, informal structure may help. Accepting and rewarding a work–life balance thing can help too.

The trouble is, for many functions a touch of O-C behavior is quite useful. The question is recognizing when enough is enough.

Online shopping

Why shop online? For many this is really an academic question where the answer is totally self-evident, namely the three Cs: *choice, cost, convenience.*

There are time and potentially financial savings to be had by shopping online. Sit in the comfort of your study without having to pay the Livingstone tax, face surly sales clerks or suffer the crowds. Ponder, peruse at leisure and pleasure. Check out the bargains, get comparative data.

Online shopping is not only convenient but helps decision-making. Online it is easy to get access to options, alternative choices. It is not only bargain-hunters who are web surfers. For many it's a lifestyle choice. Going out to shop, even for those who like it, it can sometimes be little more than tedious, time-wasting drudgery. So save time, save money.

But what do we know of the personality of online shoppers? One recent study by a team under Michael Bosnjak from Mannheim in Germany (Bosnjak *et al.* 2007) looked at this issue.

Using panel data and trying to predict annual online purchases, they tested a very specific model. First they looked at two features of a person's involvement with online shopping. Involvement of the head (how valuable, relevant and so on) and involvement of the heart (how exciting, appealing was this). Obviously more involvement meant more purchasing. So what did they think predicted involvement? Their idea was that there were four relevant needs:

- *Need for cognition* – This is the need to understand, to get involved with and to enjoy intellectual challenges. These types tend to seek out and process information before making decisions.
- *Need to evaluate* – This is the need to judge and assess and appraise. This is the "compare and contrast" need.
- *Need for arousal* – This is the need for stimulation, for excitement, for buzz. It is the strong desire to have new experiences and novelty.
- *Need for material resources* – This is quite simply the joy in accumulation; in valuing material objects; in possessing new, exciting and beautiful things.

This is the concept so far. Heavy online shoppers need to be involved in the process of shopping. And those who get involved probably have strong needs for cognition, evaluation, arousal and material resources. But what of personality? Do extraverts get bored shopping on the web? Are neurotics too worried about fraud and non-delivery to purchase this way?

The study found three personality factors were important. Open, curious, imaginative people liked shopping on the web. So did those who tended to be less emotionally stable. Perhaps the stress of shopping in the high street is greater than that of worrying about whether the goods would arrive. And online shoppers tended to be more disagreeable than agreeable. Hard-hearted, practical, get-on-with-its tended to like online shopping.

They also found that it was affective, rather than cognitive, involvement that best predicted purchasing. In short, it was all more emotional, heart-driven stuff than cool, head-driven stuff.

Online retailers need to understand their customers. They need to understand their motives and experiences and what drives them to and away from the web. To ensure loyalty they need to understand the type of people who prefer this method of shopping. They need to focus on the *pull* and *push* factors that move them away from more traditional ways of shopping.

Reference

Bosnjak, M., Galesic, M. and Tutenc, T. (2007) "Personality Determinants of Online Shopping: Explaining Online Purchase Intentions Using a Hierarchical Approach," *Journal of Business Research*, 60, 597–605.

Petty tyranny

As ever, different surveys report different findings on workplace bullying. Some suggest around half of all staff have experienced it and nearly 80 per cent have witnessed it. It apparently happens everywhere, causes distress, stress and absenteeism, lowers turnover and reduces productivity.

Is it a case of "'twas ever thus," or is it on the increase? Are bullying cases and tribunals the result of more ambulance-chasing lawyers, bored and meddling HR "professionals" and cry-baby, work-shy wimps at work?

We used to think of bullying as a playground phenomenon, not a workplace one. We also thought of it as male-on-male. Then we appeared to recognize it existed in male-dominated, blue-collar organizations, where frustrated foremen tried to get feckless workers to do their menial work.

And the national service generation certainly knew about the loudmouthed, bullying sergeant-major. Then we heard it happens to nice, middle-class people in professional settings. And then we had concept stretch: bullying was usually understood by three things: intimidation, belittlement and physical aggression. Then we had harassment, corporate incivility and "inappropriate conduct within the current gender-appropriate norms."

And now we have "petty tyranny." A new term which encompasses the concept fully. It has six facets:

- Arbitrariness and self-aggrandisement, particularly on the part of the perpetrator.
- Persistent, explicit and implicit belittling of subordinates.
- Total lack of consideration for the thoughts, needs and feelings of all others.
- Forcing conflict resolution to suit one's own purposes with little consideration of the perspectives of others.
- The discouragement of initiative on the part of others to change the way things are done.
- Non-contingent punishment which means punishment for no cause – randomly, indiscriminately, unjustly.

More for ideological than empirical reasons, some have preferred to ignore, downplay or deny the possibility that there is an identifiable profile of the *victims* of the petty tyrant. But researchers have seen clear evidence of two categories:

- The submissive employee, typically those with low confidence and esteem, prone to anxiety, introversion and increased sensitivity.
- The proactive employee who may be aggressive, overachieving, or more likely, have an unrealistic (read: aggrandizing) view of their own capabilities.

The physically weak, odd or disabled are bullied. So are those who see in a glass darkly. Trouble is, it is never certain if these characteristics are cause or consequence, though it is likely they are both.

But what of the petty tyrants? Are they inadequate, impulsive, with a lack of emotional control, insight or thoughtfulness? Are they power-crazy predators searching for the meek and mild so that they can sharpen their psychological knives? Or is it that organizational cultures – in offices, prisons, schools – explicitly or implicitly encourage bullying?

What do we know? Petty tyranny happens more in times of organizational change where there is more uncertainty, suspicion, competition for resources. It is more common in tall, hierarchical organizations. Organizations with "poor informational flow" and "insufficient empowerment" seem to engender it. Hectic, competitive organizations with rigid win–lose performance management regimes and those with much bureaucracy seem to encourage tyranny.

Of course it is possible to offer functional explanations for petty tyranny. It serves to expel unwanted employees. It establishes an unofficial pecking order and allows mobility within it. It can be a strategy for circumventing tedious rules.

Where organizations turn a blind eye to the bullying tyrant the behavior thrives. It is as if the bullies receive tacit permission. Where organizations enjoy, favor and rejoice in "tough" and autocratic leadership styles, tyrants arise.

So how to prevent petty tyranny, bullying and workplace intimidation? Ideally reduce job strain and pressure by redesigning work flow and interaction to reduce stress and scapegoating. Second, model good leadership from the top with careful selection and appraisals. Third, institute a fair, reasonable grievance procedure. Fourth, communicate what sorts of behavior are acceptable and which are not.

There will always be petty tyrants whose lack of skill and charm can lead to misery for others. The real problem lies in the concept of "petty": it can help underestimate the extent of the problem and its causes. We apply the term tyrant to monsters like Hitler and Stalin who were far from petty.

Tyranny is morally wrong. It is also in the long term deeply inefficient. That concept is more likely to serve as a wake-up call to businesspeople. Petty tyranny, through a series of processes, reduces profits. That should be sufficient to inspire people to act.

People who interview well

There are many types of interviews. Appraisal and counseling, coaching and disciplinary, selection and assessment. Few selection exercises take place without the "golden triangle" – application form, interview and references. Candidates expect interviews. Interviewers want to see the applicants.

You may be interviewed for your first school and for a CEO job. The importance of interviews is reflected in the number of interview skills courses available. There are books on how to interview as well as how to be interviewed. There are books on crafty questions to ask. And books on how to answer crafty questions. There is, in short, an interviewing industry.

The official line is that structured interviews are valid. That is, they provide accurate predictive information. They should be "competency-led," meaning that interviewers have a list of attributes they are looking for. Trained interviewers are encouraged to ask high-yield, penetrative and salient questions to obtain the information they are after.

But of course many other factors play a part. There is ample evidence of "lookism." Attractive candidates are rated more highly on all kinds of dimensions quite unrelated to physical characteristics. We also know the personality of the interviewer may play as important a role as the personality of the interviewee.

We know that interviewers differ in their ratings of a candidate. Sometimes dramatically so. Despite the fact that they supposedly have exactly the same data available, one candidate gets the thumbs up and another the thumbs down.

But what of interview "naturals"? Just as some people seem to be photogenic, so others are interview-genic. They interview very well. Rather than fearing an interview or even bothering to prepare for it some people know that as a result of their personal characteristics they will do well.

What is it about the charming, confident person who interviews well? What do they have? Call it social skills or social intelligence, call it interpersonal skills or emotional intelligence; the good interviewee is good at both "picking up signals" and managing emotions.

They are high self-monitors. They pick up the cues suggesting when to be serious and when flippant. More importantly they pick up through non-verbal behavior who is really in charge; who is more and who less impressed. They read the interview well and have the skill to present them-selves appropriately. Past masters at the skill of impression management.

By definition they are also highly adaptable. They know they have to be what the interviewers are looking for. If the interviewers want strong leadership, boldness and courage they do the Charlton Heston. If they want sobriety, integrity and due diligence, they do that.

Good interviewees have the "gift of the gab." It's all about hind legs and donkeys. They tend to be able to think on their feet, sound plausible (if only just) on practically any topic for a short while. They can think while talking. Indeed they are also quick-thinking. So it's about neural agility.

And those who don't interview well? Serious-minded introverts, techies, low-self-monitors. It's too easy to dismiss them as lacking in con-fidence, or socially unskilled. Given time, one-on-one interviews and an opportunity to think, they can and do appear highly skilled and from this they derive confidence.

The downside of the good interviewee can be their superficiality. If they can be "all things to all men," who exactly are they? They can also be highly opportunistic rather than planful. And possibly impulsive.

Sales and marketing people interview well. So do psychopaths and narcissists. That's indeed what makes them harder to detect. Actuaries and engineers don't do as well. Theirs are activities that don't come naturally. Long-distance lorry-drivers and research scientists may also come across as inadequate, even slow.

The trick is to think about the job and selection method fit. If the most crucial part of the job is persuasive sociability, then the interview may be the best way to assess it. If the job is all about perseverance, or monitoring, or detailed analysis then the interview may be much less important or useful.

Beware the garrulous, mercurial, IT specialist. And beware, too, the ruminative, slow-witted sales executive.

People who interview well have different profiles from those who don't. But because we, often erroneously, set such store by the interview, we often make classic selection errors: selecting the bad, rejecting the good.

The interview is a hall of mirrors and a theatrical encounter. It suits some very well because they can show off their skills: adaptability, charm, quick-wittedness and social skills. For those with fewer of these, albeit important, virtues, but with many and more important abilities, it can act as a serious impediment. If the core of the job involves interview-like skills, then interview them. If not, consider other selection methods.

Personality testing at work

It has now become a bit of an annual event. Journalists declare open season on management psychologists and newspapers carry a repeat or reheat article on psychometric testing at work. And the best stories are of scandalous incompetence, injustice or greed in which ideal candidates are rejected, test questions exposed as ludicrous and, worse, there is evidence of illegal or immoral discrimination.

So the story is one of evil psychologists, naïve managers and badly treated applicants. A good story or a fairy tale? A common occurrence or a rare event?

Recruiters, selectors and trainers "discovered" psychometric tests about a quarter of a century ago although they are at least a hundred years old. Publishers and management consultants pushed, peddled and praised the tests so they soon became popular. There remained cynics, skeptics and traditionalists who never trusted them and rejoiced in their publicized failures.

But this periodic coverage is really very educative for those who know little about the subject. So here are seven didactic questions with answers:

1. Why do people use psychometric tests in recruitment?

The answer is simple: to help make better people decisions. People are complicated, ambiguous, capricious. They may be hard to read. They may attempt to conceal a lot. Recruiters are trying to gauge many different things: creativity, handling pressure, integrity, punctuality, teamworking. They need reliable data to help selection. Tests *can* provide that.

Of course some may use psychometric tests because they are fashionable or they want to appear up-to-date or scientific. They may be persuaded by consultants without really understanding the tests.

2. Are tests cost-effective?

It depends, of course, on their accuracy *and* the ability (and courage) of selectors to apply their findings. The easiest way to think about cost-effectiveness is the cost of getting it wrong. Ever tried to get rid of a well-dug-in, incompetent staff member who was a bad selection decision right from the start? Ever seen someone you turned down years ago now running a successful competitor company? If you see tests as a sensible prophylactic they can seem very cost-effective.

3. Should tests be used to select in or select out?

Most recruitment (should) start with a job analysis followed by a (parsimonious, rank-ordered) list of attributes required (both necessary and sufficient) for a competent, indeed excellent jobholder. Then through interviews and tests you look for evidence of these "competencies." But what about looking for things you don't want: arrogance, dishonesty, hypochondria? Tests may help considerably with the dark-side stuff that frequently derails people.

4. Is lying or faking good on these tests frequent, easy and really a problem?

All people fake in interviews. They commit sins of omission and commission. They do self-presentation and impression-management. They do the same with their CVs. And they can fake in tests. But if they all gave the "obvious" and desirable answer there would be two consequences. First they would all give the same answer (which they patently do not). Second there would be no evidence of test validity, which there is. There are many ways to catch dissimulation (as psychometricians politely call dissembling): lie scales, forced choice (ipsative measure) using liar profiles. People are much more prone to lie in interviews, the most popular method of selection.

5. How do clients choose between tests?

There are well over ten thousand tests available yet the average (HR) manager can't name more than ten. Obviously they know what they are marketed by consultants or test publishers. Test usage is then a function of marketing, not necessarily validity. Test-peddlers of both valid and invalid tests know that clients do not know what questions to ask. People need a consumer guide, with little stars on different criteria set by honest, disinterested experts. Why haven't they done one? Litigation by rich test-publishers? Little reward for them? *Caveat emptor*. So don't blame the product if you don't know how to choose it. You need to understand (at least a little about) psychometric qualities such as reliability, validity and process and how to assess them.

6. How important is personality at work anyway?

A person's work success at any level is a function of a number of things, but five are clear: their ability, their motivation, their personality, their colleagues and the organization's processes and procedure. You need to be bright enough for the job and motivated to do it (well). You need to have a functional, shipshape, well-managed organization. No "ideal" personality profile can compensate if the other features are missing. So it's as dangerous to believe personality is all-important as it is to believe it is not at all important.

7. Does personality change over time?

Alas, not much! Go to a school reunion for evidence. Most personality and ability characteristics are hard wired. We have data on people measured 50 to 70 years apart. There is always more evidence of continuity than of change, of stability than of variability, of consistency than of inconsistency. Trauma, training and therapy can change people. But by the mid-twenties what you see is what you get. Introverts at 10 are introverts at 90 though they may have learnt to fake extraversion.

Of course personality is important at work. Of course there are more-desirable or less-desirable profiles for particular jobs. The question remains: how you choose to find out about an applicant's personality?

Politeness at work

The idea of the service–profit chain was simple. Good management led to satisfied staff, who performed great service that led to repeat custom that ensured profitability. Or something like that. What the model tried to do was explain the process by which a non-customer-facing manager had a direct impact on the bottom line in service businesses.

Part of the profit chain mantra was that people treat their customers as they are treated by their boss. Politeness begets politeness, civility begets civility, generosity begets generosity – at all levels.

People in service industries know they are in the theatre business. There is clearly a backstage and a front stage. Service is emotional labor. You have to portray a sunny disposition, a straight back, a genuine caring attitude – however you may be actually feeling. You have to be even-handed and courteous even to the most odious, passive-aggressive customer.

Going offstage offers an opportunity to let off steam, kick off your shoes, even scream at the monstrous unfairness of everything. There is, for some, a sort of restorative justice in having a good rave about the unspeakable customer on Table 9 or in seat 36B. It can provide a sense of camaraderie with the other staff. It helps draw the line between "us" and "them."

But does all this spleen-venting help? It could spill over to peers, managers, even the business's owner. It can lead to generalized bitchiness, legitimized "nyet" attitudes and passive-aggressive hostility.

You know an organization is doomed if you see service staff receiving an unhelpful and humiliating "bollocking" by senior managers in front of customers. Indeed that is often the cause of the problem in the first place. You serve as you are managed.

Recently organizational psychologists have distinguished between two types of productivity. One is, of course, the bottom-line stuff: key ratios, sales targets and so on. But the other is about morale. There are both good and bad citizens of the office. There are life-enhancing and heart-sinking colleagues. There are those who qualify for Anti-Social Behavior Orders and those who deserve medals.

Some organizations are deeply conscientious about modeling good behavior. Schools are, or should be. Teachers might call each other by their formal names: "Excuse me, Mr Gradgrind"; "Yes, Miss McChokem-child." They speak politely front stage and backstage. They show, in short, respect: that which they want, and demand, those in their care to show. They openly volunteer for tedious tasks; they behave honestly and with integrity. They lavishly praise good behavior. They bring out the sun.

Is politeness an oldfashioned word for respect, which we hear so much on the lips of those who want it, but do not show it? Many confuse "service" with "being servile" and many seem to confuse politeness with passivity or lack of assertiveness.

Polite people are agreeable. But politeness is not a trait or an ability. It is a state of mind. It is easy and important to learn. Children in all societies are "drilled" in polite etiquette that is functionally designed to make all forms of social intercourse work more effectively.

You can legislate for politeness, but it is far more important to model it, particularly in the service industries. Good service managers tend to have good service staff, which leads to customers happy to pitch up for more.

Is politeness another word for emotional intelligence or social skills? Perhaps. But it is more than the clinical management of others' emotions. It's about courtesy, another word that is not really in the social science lexicon. Pity. It's important at work.

And what about young, surly people, who apparently have all passed "Assertiveness 101," but not even taken "Charm and Manners 101"? It is a USP at work. Perhaps "natural politeness" should be on every organization's competency list.

Product knowledge may be a dangerous thing

It seems perfectly sensible to assume that all salespeople are completely familiar with all aspects of their product. They are expected to have the answers to all the clever questions, as well as the dim and the frankly daft ones, about what they are selling. What is the handle made of? Where are products sourced? Is there a helpline to provide user support? Which is the most popular model?

For some salespeople the product knowledge issue is no problem because they have chosen to sell products they are deeply interested in. Don't keen golfers open golf shops? Don't boy-racers choose to become car salesmen? Don't great cooks open restaurants?

Can there ever be any downside to sales staff being enthusiasts? Possibly, particularly if the customer does not share the same outlook.

Try a car showroom. Most of the sales staff are youngish men. And they know their stuff. Many live and breathe cars. They might not know the capital of Serbia, the plot of *Macbeth* or the way to calculate the circumference of a circle, but they know about obscure car names and numbers. They know the models well. Some probably make Clarkson look like an ignoramus.

The same pattern is found in other shops selling technical equipment. Camera and IT shops, DIY warehouses and those wonderfully oldfashioned hardware stores.

It's pretty clear what managers want from salespeople. They need to be socially skilled, attentive, energetic and robust. They need to be optimists able to cope with setbacks and hardships.

They need to be able to "read the customer" and have sales IQ. They need to be adaptable to their needs: see where they are coming from and respond appropriately. And whatever else they do, they must not "leak contempt" for the customers' taste and preferences, or worse, pooh-pooh their suggestions or choices.

Most people can describe an experience where sales or service staff intimidated them. That used to be the way the poorly paid head wine-waiter (*sommelier*) got his revenge on some *nouveau riche* wide-boy out to impress his girlfriend – the slightly raised eyebrow and snarled lip as the hapless beer-drinker chose and mispronounced the "wrong" wine to complement the food.

Women say this happens in posh dress shops; men in places of high-tech products. Try going into a specialist electronics shop that deals with computer games to buy one for a 12-year-old, mad-keen nephew. Where to begin?

The really well-informed, product-enthusiast salesperson may be a problem for three reasons. The first is that they may find it difficult to hide their contempt or pity for someone so obviously ignorant about something so important. How, they wonder, can anyone at the beginning of the twenty-first century not know, care about or use a Wii or Sony PlayStation 3? What is their problem? Are they dim, pathetic, or worse – a non-believer? Do you have to speak really simply or slowly to these people so obviously unable to keep up with modern progress? So they patronize. Not a recommended response for sales staff.

The next problem is revenge. Sales staff are often not paid well. Some even eschew better pay to be around their favorite products. A sort of labor of love. A sacrifice worth it. And some are easily made jealous of guys with thick wallets. The multiple credit card owner. The get-it-at-any cost customer. They seem naïve, gullible and childlike. Indeed their ignorance makes them unworthy of the best products. A wine waiter once refused a drunken party of businessmen one of his best bottles of claret because they were not in a state to appreciate it.

The whole point about being gullible is that on some level the client becomes an easy target. Easy to sell old stock; less popular models; low-priced tat. The purchaser does not know what questions to ask, how to specify criteria or indeed how to interrogate the salesperson. So the vengeful, greedy, product enthusiast can make an easy killing. But he or she certainly doesn't guarantee the customer loyalty or repeat purchasing. Chances are that those customers discover they have been duped and never return. Short-term gain, long-term loss.

The final problem is egocentrism. People buy and use products for many different reasons. Most never use all the fancy add-ons and special features of cars, computers and cameras. Some do: that is why they bought them. Lots don't. The sales skill is finding out what people really want the product for. Don't confuse, overwhelm or intimidate. What is their situation, what is their problem, what product will satisfy that need?

This is not an argument for not ensuring that sales staff have sufficient, up-to-date product knowledge. But it is a warning about product enthusiasm actually reducing sales skills. Enthusiasts can be geeky, snobbish, one-trackers. Not at all what you really want from sales people.

Rainbow marketing

We have the gay market and the gray market. We have the ethical market and the ethnic market. We have an avowedly Christian market and a more observable Muslim market. And of course we have the oh-so-desirable A1 market and the down-at-heel D and E markets.

There are lots of ways to segment the market, most based on old-style "breakdown" factors of age, sex and class. But the advertisers have become more aware of lifestyle marketing. This addresses groups of people who, through their hobbies and values and personal situations, make up a group.

There is, going back many years now, the "science" of *psychographics,* which aimed to provide what demographics could not, namely a psychological profiling of consumers. Most attempts took either the population as a whole or particular products (for example automobiles) or even unique brands and then tried to determine the characteristics of the distinguishable groups that bought the product. Psychographics tried to understand consumers by their lifestyle activities and opinions. And it continues to, but now looks also at values and beliefs – indeed ideology. Hence segmenting by sexual differences and preferences.

But could, or indeed should, one segment by political values? Is there a red or a blue market? Look at the ads in the *Daily Telegraph* and *Daily Mail* and contrast them with the *Guardian* or the *Sun*. Or is this readership analysis simply too confounded by age and social class?

So who are – what is – the blue market? Blue team: Conservatives and conservationists. Oldfashioned people with oldfashioned values. Old fogies, middle-England, salt-of-the-earth? How to appeal to the blues? Well, there is patriotism. The British flag on meat products; the lion on eggs; those marvelous "By Appointment" crests. Team Blue are patriots: proud of it and happy to buy products that show it. They are also probably nostalgic. After all conservatism is derived from conserve. They like the traditional, the oldfashioned and are not fashion-conscious.

Value for money, reliability and functionality are blue criteria. They are, no doubt, less interested in new technology, exclusivity or exotic foreign labels.

And Team Red? Well, it's probably important to differentiate Old vs. New Labour. They may be polls (or perhaps Poles) apart in their tastes.

Remember, Old Labour like mushy peas while New Labour eat guacamole. New Labour is (was?) hip. International. Citizens of cool Britannia. But although they may be declining in numbers they are at least happy to wear the badge.

There is the very observable and growing "green" pound. The wind is behind the Greenies. Greenness *de rigueur* for young people. They are the Fairtrade buyers, and Fairtrade is a concept quite foreign to the value-for-money brigade. They want to avoid overpackaging and enjoy recycling. Some favor local over foreign. They want to know about the food miles. They are aware of food additives and colorings and genetic modification.

The green purchasers have more indignation than the other colored groups. Every shopping expedition potentially "saves the earth." They shop to help the future of mankind. They don their moral armor when setting off for grocery stores.

There is also the black and brown pound. Some products are designed for very specific ethnic needs. Skin and hair products are obvious, but there are others. Often there are religious connotations too. No doubt in Northern Ireland there is an orange pound, similar to the blue, but nicely distinct. And the yellow pound of that quietly industrious and very successful Chinese/Japanese community. Certainly they have specialist food products, but also seem very logo-conscious.

Does this color-coding work for marketing people? Perhaps, if it helps identify and target certain groups. Sometimes it's simply too crude, too inclusive, too vague. But it does draw attention to an important mix of lifestyle and values that powerfully influences shopping habits and buying preferences.

Reactions to organizational change

There is a wonderful prayer from the monastic office of Compline: "Be present, O merciful God, and protect us through the silent hours of this night, so that we who are fatigued by the changes and chances of this fleeting world may repose upon thy eternal changelessness." The word change is both boring and anxiety-provoking: the former because you keep hearing it; the latter because it usually means pain of one sort or another.

Inevitably, organizations are most concerned with resistance to change, which will be manifest in everything from strikes and sabotage through a drop in motivation and morale to no participation in, and commitment to, change initiatives. The clever ones anticipate anti-change agents and try to "push change through" as effectively as they can.

Organizational change causes powerful emotions from a sense of liberation to depression and humiliation. People's support of, or resistance to, change depends heavily on how they answer the following questions:

- Will this change cause me to gain or lose something of value?
- Do I understand the nature of this change?
- Do I trust the initiators of this change?
- Do I agree with the advisability of this change?
- Given my personality, personal values, and attitudes, how do I feel about this change?

How they answer these questions may lead to one of seven responses:

- *Quitting* – The most extreme reaction an employee shows to a change is to leave the organization. For example, following the introduction of a major organizational change, such as a merger or a transfer in job assignment, many workers leave because they believe the change is so obnoxious that staying would be intolerable. Sometimes organization members depart even if the change is a good one, because they find it personally difficult to cope with the change. *Early retirement* is a convenient and acceptable way to dismiss people who are unhappy with organizational change. Some prefer generous *voluntary severance payment*, though it is not always voluntary. Although leaving an organization may be the most extreme reaction to change, it is not necessarily the most damaging one to the organization. Indeed, things probably proceed more smoothly if the most adamant opponents of a change leave rather than stay to fight it. Dare one admit that some changes, like restructuring, are designed specifically to encourage (certain) people to leave?

- *Active resistance* – Workers who actively resist a change may try either to prevent it from occurring or to modify its nature. At its extreme, active resistance sends the message "No, I will not do this." Active resistance often goes beyond personal defiance and includes attempts to encourage others to resist the change. Many organizational changes have been scuttled by active employee resistance. A strike is a good example of group-orientated active resistance, though these days there are all sorts of other, clever ways to drum up support for one's cause and disrupt the whole change process.

- *Opposition* – This is somewhat less extreme than active resistance. Usually somewhat passive in nature, opposition behavior might result in no more than simple "foot-dragging" to delay implementation or to bring about a scaled-down version of a proposed change. Opposition is a tactic commonly used by those who control resources that are necessary for the change to be made. By withholding essential resources, people can slow or modify a change quietly without having to make their dislike for the change known actively or aggressively. This is the preferred approach of the pusillanimous passive-aggressive worker.

- *Acquiescence* – Opposition reactions tend to occur when those affected dislike a change and engage in passive resistance to delay or modify it. Sometimes, however, those opposed to a change feel powerless to prevent or alter it and they allow the change to occur without interference. This acquiescence to an unwanted change may arise from an impending sense of its inevitability – like death or taxes. People put up with the inevitable as best they can, shrugging their shoulders, gritting their teeth, and steeling themselves to face the inevitable. They hardly welcome the change but understand its inevitability. It is the stoical way.

- *Acceptance/modification* – Employees who demonstrate an acceptance/ modification response accept a change to a certain extent but have some reservations about it. For example, suppose a manager has been told that her employer intends to move the company's headquarters to another

European capital. She supports the idea of moving operations because local taxes and other restrictive ordinances are hurting the company's ability to compete in the marketplace. On the other hand, she is worried that the change may alienate many of its major customers and adversely affect supply and delivery systems. At a personal level, she would rather not move her family too far from friends and relatives. One option available is to try to persuade her employer that there are sound reasons for finding a different site in the same country. Acceptance/modification responses to change usually can be characterized as bargaining over details (albeit perhaps important ones), rather than over principles.

- *Acceptance* – This type of reaction is likely when either people are indifferent towards the change (that is, they do not actually *dislike* it), or they agree with it. Acceptance reactions to change are characterized by passive lukewarm support. If asked whether they like the change, for example, workers might agree that they do – but they are unlikely to volunteer such information. If asked to participate in the change, they will cooperate – but they probably will not initiate participation. They may see change as inevitable or that their jobs ultimately depend on it. It is often the logical head and the passionate heart: the former is logical and reasonable and knows the situation. The latter wishes to continue without the change.

- *Active support* – In this situation, organization members choose to engage actively in behaviors that increase the change's chances of success. Active supporters often initiate conversations, explaining why they support the change and think it is a good idea. They embrace, welcome and even rejoice in change. The are usually young or have a lot to gain – or are somewhat naïve!

All people tend to become satisfied with the *status quo*. Insecurity develops when changes occur. Sometimes this insecurity is caused by economic factors. Lower-level workers fear that automation will result in unemployment. Higher-level employees might view change as a threat to their status and eventually to their economic wellbeing.

The following is a checklist of factors that account for why people don't change, although it may be in their best interests, resisting for various reasons:

- *Because of ignorance* – Often, concerned individuals are simply not aware of the changes taking place.

- *By default* – Sometimes people may reject a change, even though they are aware of another better technique, with little justification except a desire not to learn to use a new method.
- *On the basis of the status quo* – Change is rejected because it will alter the way in which things have traditionally been done.
- *Because of social reasons* – A manager may refuse to change because of a rationalization that the people within, and society outside, the organization will not accept it.
- *On the basis of interpersonal relations* – Because friends and even competitors have not accepted the change or are threatened by it.
- *Through substitution* – Another process or technique is selected in favor of the proposed change, because it seems easier, safer and less threatening.
- *Because of experience* – People reject a change when they try it but do not like it, or do it badly, wrongly or half-heartedly, thus self-fulfilling their prophesies.
- *Through incorrect logic* – People may reject a change on supposedly "logical" grounds without having well-founded reasons. Collective rationalization is strong when passion is involved.

In short, people resist change through habit and the inconvenience of having to do things differently. Fearing the unknown, insecurity or indeed economic implications (having to work harder) are main causes of individuals resisting change. All organizations are in a state of equilibrium as a consequence of various forces, some pushing for change and others resisting it. Managers have to attempt to identify *all* the salient forces for and against change, and next identify those that seemed controllable. Once the most important controllable forces are identified, they could attempt first to unfreeze the organization by reducing the forces holding the behavior in the organization as stable; attempt next to change structures and procedures; and then attempt to refreeze by stabilizing the organization at a new state of equilibrium.

Research workers

A witty academic remarked once that research was a bit like praying. It is a private, very respectable, but essentially pointless activity. Research can be used as a verb or noun. You research an issue to understand it, to find out what others have thought about it.

And there are professional researchers. Big companies have a research and development department. Universities have many people with the "R" word in their title. Indeed the R-word is better than the T-word (teacher). Research is all about discovery, about things new, about activity. Teaching may be worthy, but by comparison it is rather dull.

Research itself can take on many characteristics. Conducted in labs or libraries, alone or in teams. More important is the aim of the activity. Is it a scientific paper that practically nobody will read, or is it a medical cure that will benefit millions? People research what for many sounds trivial. Which color M&Ms do kids prefer? What should the name be of a new vodka or computer? And that leads to a rather lowlier form of the art: market research. People who stand outside grocery stores interviewing you about an everyday product you have little knowledge of, or indeed care much about.

What drives people to the research world? Is it their curiosity or perhaps their lack of social skills? We celebrate scientists who seem to live for their work. And we often admire people who endure pain and hardship along with poverty. To the outsider they can look alike with their poor dress sense, their fixation with gadgets and their apparent (and irreversible) charisma bypass. But to the trained eye there are clear differences between them. Consider the following typology:

Chronicler – The one who logs, records and monitors to make sure nothing is forgotten, omitted or distorted. He (or She) is the memory of the past: keeping people on track and eager to avoid re-inventing the wheel.

Challenger – This is the fearless interviewer, "unafraid" to ask the really important question of the great and the good. Often the most naïve questions are the most piercing. No matter who said what and when, the challenger wants to hear exactly what things mean.

Clarifier – The clarifier is the enemy of big-picture, enthusiastic flim-flam. He wants to know precisely how much things cost; how they will work; who will be responsible. They are often a thorn in the side of those who paint a bean-counter image with large, undeliverable promises.

Checker – Someone needs to know how things are progressing. These are the monitor evaluators of the R & D world. They need to have their ducks in a row, for the supply line to be clear, for the emergency procedures to be in place.

Classifier – These are the stamp-collectors of the world, with happy mottoes for "everything in its place." They are made deeply anxious and uncomfortable if things are not put where they should be. This extends from apostrophes to pencils, disks to (especially) papers. "A tidy desk," they are heard to say "reflects a tidy mind."

Champion – These are the spokespeople of R&D. They are the "Tomorrow's World" wannabes who can paint compelling pictures of the new Jerusalem, where labor is abolished along with illness, pain and drudgery. They champion the future, the power of science and technology. Some can even be inspiring.

Change agent – It is the D part of R&D that implies moving on. Development is about change. The change agent sees change as inevitable and highly desirable. They scorn those wedded to old technologies, to old ways of thinking. They see nothing bar a happy future. Some can get really nasty if you don't share their views.

Of course researchers are an odd lot. And they do make spectacular cock-ups and bad decisions. Remember Sinclair's C5. Remember the millennium bug that would cause computers to go haywire, planes to fall out of the sky.

But they need to be nurtured and respected. Yes they are frequently Asberger's spectrum-like in their social behavior. Yes, they can seem to be difficult or unproductive for long periods. But all successful manufacturers, particularly of drugs and technology, know they are essential to the health of the business.

Sales intelligence

The multiple intelligence industry began over twenty years ago with an academic called Howard Gardner. In fact his central tenet that intelligence is not one central, core attribute goes back nearly a hundred years. Everyone agrees that you can divide up intelligence into specific component parts, but the question remains whether they are related or not. Do bright people tend to do well on all of them and dim ones on none? Or can you be very good at some intellectual tasks and very weak at others?

The multiple intelligence enthusiasts love the idea that all can have prizes. You might have done poorly at school, be poor at crosswords or sudoku, find it hard to read maps or add up grocery bills, but still have a large, generous dollop of bodily-kinesthetic or spiritual intelligence.

Two gurus fought the multiple intelligence war, but the one who listed the most types of intelligence won. Indeed he was so rewarded that he has been on the treasure hunt ever since. He has found three more types of intelligence, including existential and naturalistic intelligence, but seems confident only with the latter.

And this has unleashed a frenzy of intelligence-hunters. Some have found sexual intelligence, others political intelligence. At work individuals might possess networking intelligence or negotiation intelligence. But the prize goes to Goleman, who combined two intelligences – intra- and interpersonal intelligence – into *emotional intelligence*. Others had used the idea – in fact it can be traced back many years – but he touched a nerve.

We have all worked with very bright people. Those who sailed through high school, university and an MBA by doing the hard subjects: math, physics, chemistry. They can tumble numbers with ease; spot trends; model processes and draw up impressive strategic plans. But they seem not to be able to motivate and inspire others. They appear to be all head and no heart; all data and analysis but very little understanding of what makes people tick.

So is what they need emotional intelligence? What is this semi-mysterious but all-conquering quality? Two things: *understanding* how emotions work in yourself *and* others, and then being able to *manage* emotions – that is, change them. So you need to be perceptive and flexible, sensitive and skillful.

Emotional intelligence: Your dad called it charm; you understood it as social skill; the trainers now call it EQ. A useful concept, or just repackaged common sense?

Certainly "an intelligence" is an up-market concept. Nice to have one. Bit like an NVQ. So why not? And why not make it job-specific?

So why not *sales intelligence?* The essential attributes of a good sales-person. A sort of psychological job specification. And it must be closely associated with emotional intelligence. Selling is more about emotion than intellect. You sell dreams, benefits, solutions.

Sales people need to be emotionally literate. They need to pick up signals from their clients, to read them well. And they need to be really self-aware and insightful about their own emotions. However, perhaps more than either of these, the heart of sales intelligence is the management of the whole sales encounter that leads to the magical "closing the deal" stage.

And yet the most important sales management issue is the self. Most people say no. The question then is managing disappointment and rejection. Salespeople have to remain upbeat, optimistic and energetic in the face of consistent setbacks. They need to be highly resilient, highly determined, seriously goal-focused.

So yes, if you are keen on finding new intelligences, there probably is something called sales intelligence *if* you are happy to include a package of dispositions and skills under this rubric. But it does open the thorny question of whether you can acquire sales intelligence, or whether you have to be born with it.

The satnav market

Satnav is a must-have. But is it a sexy, flash-in-the-pan toy, or a serious bit of business kit no one can do without? Clearly the latter. And dare one say it: particularly useful for the fairer sex, demonstrably shown to be less good on a range of spatial tasks like map-reading? Or perhaps the travelling rep who can't drive and map-read simultaneously?

Once you have learnt to work the darn thing it makes trips to unfamiliar parts a joy. You really know the meaning of autopilot when you have confidence that nanny will tell you precisely where to go.

It's odd to believe that orbiting spacecraft designed for the cold war are helping you around the backstreets of Tooting Bec and that satellites in space know precisely how to get around East Cheam.

There are different models of satnav; and there are already different options. You can change the voice. So you might feel more confident with a BBC Radio 4 announcer voice or a Joanna Lumley. You might be more at home with a West Midlands or Tyneside accent, or perhaps a character from Star Wars?

But the satnav designers have so far missed a trick. They have not yet designed specialized or customized satnav systems for particular kinds of drivers. We know people drive as they live. And we know that people lead very different lives.

Designers, manufacturers and marketers soon learn to segment markets. They build up psychographic and demographic profiles of their customers and provide different products for their different needs.

So what about satnav? Intuitively, it appears that five or six different models need to be designed to address different market segments.

- *The nervous driver* – Insecure, anxious, prone to depression and moody, the nervous driver needs reassurance. Satnav could be a counseling device. So once the mailing code is inputted it might say: "Go on – you can do it!" Or you could have the non-directive one: "How did you feel about that junction?" After each correct execution of the left or right turn, how about "Well done; you're doing well." The worst times are when the voice goes silent in the long bits where you are required just to follow the road. These may easily be interpreted as cold, judgmental silences, where nanny is not really approving of your driving skill. So here we need the counselor's reassurance that all is well. Thus every minute, at least, we need "We are doing well!" "Excellent progress!" and "Not far now, nearly there!" And the destination must also involve therapeutic positive feedback psychobabble.

- *The boy-racer* – This needs a "Clarkson" voice and attitude. "At the next junction turn left" becomes "hang a left." "Straight on" becomes "Give it the gun barrel." The boy racer wants to know how and when and where to go faster. The trip is a game, a challenge to manhood – a hunt. So the voice needs to be programmed to flatter the road-holding, cornering, smooth acceleration and smart overtaking of cautious Lada drivers. The satnav must be a mate not a crutch. It must do blokey non-PC talk. "Get a move on, china" or "Get your ass into gear for the next traffic circle." Jolly good fun to write the script. A surefire seller.

- *The obsessional* – The quality-control, health-and-safety-type driver wants exact detail and more feedback than machines currently supply. None of this "in 800 yards" vagueness. "In 820 yards" is much better. Obsessionals need to get it right: first time and exactly. So once they have programmed the machine, they need to know they have done it correctly. The voice should repeat and confirm the destination. Some obsessionals need to know their general direction, so how about: "In 745 yards turn left (an 11 o'clock turn), so that we are now proceeding east-southeast on the A204 to Great Winterbottom. The road, first constructed in 1947, has recently been resurfaced and has excellent grip." Some obsessionals might like to know a frequent and continuously updated time of arrival. The voice should be clear and exacting. Remember obsessionals have concerns with time, cleanliness, orderliness and parsimony. Build it in.

- *The rap artist* – There must be a warning on the box because rap is, for some, a foreign tongue. It may be the hardest model to build. But it is not difficult to imagine the rap voice on start up: "Yo! Let's move it!" or the instruction to maneuver "You turn to the right, along the road outta sight – cool." And if a mistake is made, the indignant "Hey, man! What's going on here? You are doin' my head in with this stuff! Get with it, will ya." Obviously the rap satnav would be the hardest to build, needing specialized input from young people at the cutting edge, and almost daily updates to keep abreast of the latest, ever-changing slang. But an appealing concept nevertheless, if only to baffle the oldies in the passenger seats.

So there you have it: a starter set of five satnav "personalities," which different types of driver could identify with. But why stop there? If it is possible to think of multiple variations on a theme, or a "learning satnav" which builds up an individual's profile according to performance of different dimensions when it goes on an outing (for example mistakes made, time to destination and so on).

And, ultimately, why not have a satnav option as individual as your ring tone?

Segmenting shoppers

There have been many attempts to develop a typology of shoppers. Learned papers have appeared on the topic for over fifty years. Some have been based on actual shoppers, some on "heads of household" and some more recently on internet users. Some researchers conduct "in-depth interviews," others telephone polls, but the majority rely on questionnaires. And each method has its limitations.

While they all make interesting reading and there is clearly some overlap between the categories and the descriptors, there remains no agreed taxonomy or list of prototype shoppers for all products. Thus one study of departmental store shoppers in the 1950s claimed evidence of three types (dependent, compulsive, individualistic), while another study twenty years later was able to differentiate between seven different types, labeled as apathetic, demanding, quality, fastidious, store-card preferer, convenience, and store card hater.

The researchers have been rather creative with their labels. One study of cosmetic buyers had *psycho-socializing types* and *name-conscious types*, while another, of housewives, found four types – namely indifferent, oldfashioned, healthy brigade, and hedonistic.

Of course, shopper segmentation does depend on *who* they are, *where* they shop and *what* they are looking for. And, naturally, the results depend also on your method of research. What people say, what they do in shops and what products they buy are not the same and do yield different typologies. And thirdly, rather a lot depends on the sample – its size, composition and honesty.

This research has definitely been getting more sophisticated. A recent paper in the *Journal of Retailing and Consumer Services* (Bandyopadhyay and Martell 2007) derived a practical and sensible segmentation. The authors found evidence of just six types that could easily and usefully be further segmented. They were:

- *Choice-optimizers* – These are authoritative, brand-conscious, individualistic inquirers. They ask questions, read labels, process information. They are often fully involved in the process: they make comparisons, query product, quality and performance criteria and are clearly quality-conscious. They are at best thoughtful and informed, but sales staff see them as difficult, demanding and possibly dithering.

- *Economizing* – These are pretty clear: bargain- and discount-seeking, budget- and price-conscious. Some try negotiating and bargaining to reduce prices. They switch brand, being price-fixated. The price tag rules all. The bargain basement is their destination. And they can be very vocal if "the price is not right." You certainly know where you stand with this group.

- *Premeditated* – These are the hurried, list-driven, predecided. They are often the family bulk-buyers. They are restless, goal-driven, get-up-and-go-types. They come for a purpose, they don't linger, or ponder or dither. They often ask salespeople for a specific product on their list and trouble them for little else.

- *Recreational* – this is the sauntering, browsing roamer who appears to wander around shops aimlessly soaking up their ambience. They seem to be killing time, often with friends or relatives. They can be very vocal in their reactions to products, treating the whole event as somewhere between a street market and street theatre. They can make quite impulsive buys but often buy nothing at all. "Just browsing, thank you."

- *Low-information-seeker* – They may be opposites in the sense that they are very familiar or very infrequent visitors. They may just pop in for the same product every time or they may be very unsure, not of the product, but of where to go and what to do.

- *Support-seeker* – The final type, self-conscious and indecisive. They seem intimidated by shops, being self-conscious, submissive and nervous. They may come accompanied by a friend who is very frequently consulted for advice, but more often approval. They seem to need therapy and encouragement from all around them, especially the sales staff. They worry about exchanging the object, about guarantees, about anything that could go wrong.

The authors believe that more females are choice-optimizers: perhaps a third of all shoppers. The premeditated and the low-information-seekers tend to shop alone rather than be accompanied.

And what about shopper types in relation to product categories? Choice-optimizers are very noticeable in cosmetics, books and music. The premeditated seem most preponderant in apparel and medicine. Groceries and durables are the world of the economizing, while support-seekers seem to need most help with gifts, cards and shoes. Low-information-seekers are common in the grocery, medicine and apparel sections. The recreational only make up 7.5 per cent of the market, but it is bookstores and music stores that draw them.

Clearly how retailers train their staff, display their wares and lay out their stores should reflect their predominant customer types. Perhaps that is why bookstores have coffee shops and cosmetic counters can be so heavily staffed.

Reference

Bandyopadhyay, S. and Martell, M. (2007) "Does Attitudinal Loyalty Influence Behavioral Loyalty? A Theoretical and Empirical Study," *Journal of Retailing and Consumer Services*, *14*, 35–44.

Sex and money

Despite longstanding antidiscrimination legislation there remains a gender earnings gap. Overall, women earn less than men. Researchers, policymakers and journalists ask why that should be.

The economists have conducted various wage composition studies and found that in many countries men tend to have more education, experience and qualifications than women.

Some would be bold enough to argue that specialist male cognitive abilities (that is math) are more valuable in the marketplace than female abilities (that is emotional intelligence).

But the evidence for sex differences in ability is both controversial and equivocal. If there are differences they are very small and where they occur (that is spatial intelligence) they do not seem to relate to getting a well-paid job.

Of course, there are a number of sociopolitical explanations for the sex difference in income which are essentially about entrenched subtle discrimination of one sort or another. Hence the metaphors about glass ceilings, glass escalators, glass cliffs and the like.

There are other explanations for the phenomenon. The most obvious is child-rearing. However well qualified she may be, having a couple of children in her thirties may well mean a woman is out of the rat race for two to five (or more) crucial years when it is necessary to fight the opposition to achieve prominence. Further, in some worlds, rapid changes in technology mean that you surprisingly quickly become out-of-date in skills and understanding.

It has also been argued that women are clever and wise enough not to choose a stressed, well-paid life over a less hectic, less frenetic and slower-paced life with less money. They see the game as not worth the candle. That is, they choose less well-paid work deliberately.

Or is it personality? There are proven, albeit small, sex differences in personality. Women tend to be less adjusted, more prone to anxiety, depression and worry. They don't cope as well with stress. Therefore they fail more frequently. Therefore they tend to be in less stressful senior jobs and are paid less accordingly.

Two other personality-type factors seem to be implicated in gender differences and in correlates of wealth accumulated. One is called *instrumentalism* or internal locus of control. It is the belief that one is in charge of one's fate or destiny, captain of one's ship, master of one's fate. People with this attribute tend to be more motivated, optimistic and have greater initiative. The second is called *need for challenge* or the desire to get ahead of others. People with this trait are competitive, success-oriented and tend to "get ahead" of the competition.

A recent study in the *Journal of Economic Psychology* attempted to test this hypothesis based on Russian data collected over a four-year period. The authors, economists at an American university, found that men had a greater internal locus of control and a greater need for challenge, while women had a more external (fatalistic) locus of control and more need for affiliation. They found that personality did affect earnings, but more for women than men. Personality alone accounted for almost 10 per cent of the earnings gap.

To some extent these results are self-explanatory. Those who have more need for challenge and are driven to get ahead do better than those who have a greater need for affiliation and are motivated to "get along" with others So being competitive, egocentric and focused on one's career pays off.

Equally the finding that instrumentalists do better than fatalists is hardly surprising. The former believe in "making" their luck, not being "victims" of it. They believe they have control and exercise it. "Externals" are too passive, waiting for things to happen to them because they believe in chance and fate.

But these are not strictly personality variables in the biological sense. They are cognitive variables – perhaps belief variables – which are socialized into people. Men are taught to compete as individuals or in teams, women to cooperate.

The results of the study do suggest that personality factors are more important for women. Competitive, instrumental – that is, less "traditional" – women are more likely to achieve earnings similar to those of men than are cooperative, more traditional women.

So is it all discrimination? No it's largely socialization. The Freudians and the Jesuits were right. It's all about childhood and adolescence where these attitudes and beliefs are firmly entrenched, and have their impact later in life.

Reference

Semykina, A. and Linz, S. J. (2007) "Gender Differences in Personality and Earnings: Evidence from Russia," *Journal of Economic Psychology*, 28(3), June, pp. 387–410.

Span of control

It was Max Weber, the father of bureaucracy, that most misunderstood of managerial concepts, who specified a few crucial organizational structural variables. Two have been under threat for a long time: chain of command and span of control.

Perhaps it is not at all unhealthy to challenge long-held beliefs and practices. Some challenges, such as the evidence-based school, are to be welcomed. Others, like the naïve modernization school, are less useful.

Weber argued that it is crucial to understand the *chain of command*– essentially who reports to whom. This should be clear, open and logical. Everyone should know who their boss is and be clear about their role in relation to them.

He also believed that there was a clear limit to the number of people any one individual could reasonably successfully manage. This he termed the *span of control*. The precise number depends on the nature of the jobs people are expected to perform and the necessity of close and consistent supervision.

The military everywhere have rarely doubted these simple but profound principles. Even the most radical and clearly mad leaders like Pol Pot or Stalin consistently applied them. They may have murdered the officer class, purged all possible enemies and appointed henchmen without experience, but they left the structures in place.

As a result military forces everywhere are surprisingly similar and have always been thus. They are divided into manageable size units: platoons, companies, brigades and so on, of roughly similar size. Each is commanded by an individual to whom a set number report. They make up a team.

The question then refers to the optimal span of control. In short, how many people can one individual reasonably manage? Part of the answer must depend on what people are doing. How closely do they need to be supervised, monitored or encouraged?

When workers are highly skilled and disciplined or where the coordination of individuals is not particularly crucial, there can be a large span of control. Thus, an orchestra is very flat. Given what people do, the conductor's job is mainly coordination.

Some organizations are very flat because staff are intrinsically motivated, well trained and functionally independent. A good example is the Church or a traditional university. Both have flat structures with as many as 20 to 40 people reporting to one person.

At the other end of the scale is the apprenticeship model of skill transfer. Here the master craftsmen pass on their skills slowly to very few pupils, who observe their masters by working closely with them. It's a luxury, but one that has proved to work well.

So why are some businesses in the same sector, with essentially the same product or service, so different in the tallness of their organizations, which is often a function of span of control? Some have over 20 levels or grades, some as few as 6. Why?

Levels are often a function of history, not a function of logic or analysis. Some organizations cave in to demands from staff for advancement and rapid promotion. Flat organizations are usually characterized by slow advancement.

If staff want rapid promotion and fancy titles, some organizations simply divide up jobs into different levels. So you can be a junior, senior, executive or master cook, tea-boy, manager or salesperson.

The way to tell whether structure is a function of vanity is to look at the organogram or organizational chart. That details the span of control at each level. And it may be that fancy titles really mean little.

The magic number for highly "supervised" groups is 7, plus or minus 2. And sometimes because of the nature of skill transfer the span of control may be one or two, as in the famous Oxford tutorial.

So flattening organizations should not be a fashionable, guru-led activity. It all depends on what task people are doing and how well it has to be done.

Sudden departures

What happens when the (very visible and very successful) boss leaves? What is the effect on the corporate climate? Do all replacements receive a "honeymoon" period? And what is the role of succession planning in the whole thing?

The King is dead: God save the King. Most organizations wish for a smooth, seamless transfer of power when people at the top change, particularly if a well-liked and respected leader leaves.

In most organizations it is the (relatively) powerless who have to be particularly sensitive to the whims and peculiarities of the (relatively) powerful. Slaves need to read the mood of their master more than vice versa. And they need to adapt to their preferences.

All individuals have their little idiosyncrasies at work. Some favor email over face-to-face contact. Some court publicity, others eschew it. Some trust only that "inner circle" of confidants; others are more open. Some can't do spreadsheets; others can't write speeches. And everyone around them adjusts to their preferences. The oddest things can seem normal after a time. And they appear odd only when a new person arrives with a very different set of needs, habits and skills.

After a few years you know where you stand with your boss. So do the shareholders and the City. Nice to have a "safe pair of hands" guiding the ship into deep, calm and profitable waters. Better still if the person is genuinely liked and admired; honest and inspiring; visible and versatile.

The problem for the successor is to make their presence felt. They have a hundred days to make their mark, set their agenda and brush with a new broom. Some cause absolute mayhem, wantonly destroying all the great works of their predecessors. It is the old alpha-male lion killing all the cubs of the senior females.

The orthodox way to cope with all these eventualities is the process called *succession management*. The idea, for the top executives, goes something like this. At a certain point, which is very unclear, it becomes important to think about who will succeed key players. A shortlist maybe drawn up comprising mainly or exclusively in-house people who should or might or could be promoted to this position through their talent, loyalty, energy or some combination of very desirable competencies. And, in the fullness of time, a group of wise people select and groom the heir to the throne so that the handover is seamlessly natural and successful.

But this begs many questions. Who does this job: HR, the board, consultants or some heady mix of these? How much time and effort and money should be spent on this activity, proportional to the candidate's salary? How long should the shortlist be (ideally)? Should those being replaced ever be consulted about their successors? Should the plan be made public? Can it be revised? Should the successor shadow the boss at all? And if so for how long? What, in short, puts the success in succession?

Important questions with important implications. Sometimes companies are caught out.

A few years ago the CEO of McDonald's dropped dead while giving a speech. He was young and active and new. The company dealt with this brilliantly. His successor was in place the next day and things went on steadily.

The trainer effect

Most of us have had at least one teacher, perhaps more, who changed our lives. They fired our youthful imaginations, brought the subject alive, gave us confidence in our particular abilities.

This "special teacher" experience probably led us to choose the subject for A levels; possibly even read it at university. And sometimes it was all a mistake, because we failed to differentiate *what* was taught from *who* taught it.

Other teachers or university lecturers, however brilliant and accomplished, somehow did not have the same knack. "Our" special teacher had something unique which seemed to go beyond the discipline, a sense of which is captured in the movie *Dead Poets Society*.

The same issue is found in therapy. Wags call it "the rapist" (therapist) effect. Study after study has shown that it's not the "py" but the "pist" which has the power. The power, the efficacy, the uniqueness, lies not in whether you are couched by a Freudian, Jungian, Adlerian or even a rat-trainer, but in the chemistry between you.

The only way to sort out the effect of *what* people do/say vs. *who* does it is to ensure that the same teachers/therapists teach different subjects or give different types of therapy. So the brilliant English master needs to teach math or geography and the sensitive Freudian to do a spot of cognitive behavior therapy. Difficult, artificial, indeed almost impossible, to achieve.

It's an important question at work because it's exactly the same issue with training effectiveness. Is the success or failure of a training program dependent on *what* is trained or *who* does the training? Does it depend on where the training occurs; *when* it takes place or even *why?*

People who sponsor training courses are pressurized to justify costs, to get a spot of ROI. In short to show, if at all possible, that it has an impact on the bottom line. It's a reasonable question, but it's far from simple to answer.

Trainers rely on other forms of evaluation. The most common is the "happy sheet," on which are ratings of "the course." They might look for some behavioral data, such as how differently people behave back on the job – for example they conduct better appraisals; give better speeches; solve more problems. Or they may rely on behavioral reports. Thus subordinates, peers and clients might be asked to comment on what they noticed when X returned from a course.

But once again there is the issue of untangling the trainer from the training. Some trainers are clearly charismatic, inspirational, motivational. With passion and humor, they tell stories and anecdotes to capture the imagination. They make people want to "go back and make a difference." They make complicated things clear; difficult things simple; opaque things transparent.

Training and consultancy companies, of course, search out these individuals. They are gold dust. Being so well received, they ensure repeat business. And they can easily sell "add-ons" such as other courses or modules.

Some of these people have been teachers or in sales in the past. They intuitively know what the job is all about. It's not about the sexiness of manuals or PowerPoint slides. And it's not about the course philosophy or structure – though all those things count. It is about engagement.

The first step is to gauge the beliefs, motives, abilities of the "delegates", to find out who is "in today." Then speak their language at their pace with (if possible) stories from their world. Don't ever patronize them, but do stretch them. Give them an idea of what is possible, what it will mean and that they can achieve it.

Is "trainer magic" a personality trait, an ability or some sort of gift? Bright, agreeable, extraverts, or more prosaically dedicated, hard-working individuals with a vocation?

Training is hard work. It's tiring and relentless. Those who are good at training find their skills in high demand elsewhere, on the "after-dinner speech circuit" or other areas of the "performing arts."

The trouble is, brilliant trainers aren't hard to spot. Or manage. But they may be hard to retain.

TV blues

We have more leisure time than ever. And how do we fill it? Bettering the mind; family outings; restoring the soul? Charitable work, keep fit, even DIY? No. Watching television. Studies conducted in both Europe and America over the past forty years have shown a steady, linear increase in daily time spent watching television. We watch round about three hours per day. Figures from different studies are surprisingly consistent. Like it or not, deny it or not, we spend one eighth of the day watching the box.

But let's not do all that snobbish, middle-class, television-watching guilt scenario. Television can inform, educate, and amuse. The questions is how enjoyable it is relative to other leisure time activities. This can be tested by what is called "experience sampling." A person carries a bleeper which goes off randomly at various times of the day. At that point they have to record what they are doing, feeling and thinking.

People watch television for many reasons: entertainment, education, relaxation. It seems to offer many benefits at very low cost. Some multi-task with the television on. But do people watch too much, as many frequently admit? Do they trade off beneficial physical exercise, or socializing or indeed doing important chores for passive, even mindless, devotion to the box?

A central, albeit simple, question is whether television watching makes us happy. Surveys – one recent study was of 42,000 Europeans from 22 countries – suggest the answer is no. Excessive TV watchers report, on average, lower life satisfaction. But this is correlational, not causal. It could be that unhappy people watch TV, not that watching causes the former. Or there could be many other factors that produce this correlation: poorer people in menial jobs are more unhappy and have only enough money to watch television as an amusement or leisure pursuit. Or old, ill, depressed people can't get out and have television as their only company.

Happiness is about life satisfaction. This is shaped by many different factors. Sex, age, marital status, health, education and job. And people have a choice as to how they prefer to spend their leisure time. That is why questions about preferred leisure crop up in interviews. The assumption is that you get to know the real person when you know how they spend their leisure.

Of course, there are constraints on leisure activities. Some are very expensive, some demand facilities (like snowy mountains or green fields). But the real issue is interpretation.

Nobody puts television-watching as their primary leisure behavior although it is, in effect, for many. Why not? Television can inform, educate and amuse. But it is thought by some to be a lazy, passive and antisocial activity. Recall stentorian middle-class statements rejoicing in their television setlessness. Children are rationed with regard to TV. We all bemoan the lowering of standards, repeats, endless copycat cooking programs.

But what do a person's TV habits really say about them? Do introverts watch more than extraverts because the latter prefer live interaction? Do the less able watch while the more able read? Do the anxious watch more because they are afraid to go out?

Or does it depend on the program and time of day? If a person follows a soap opera, or is addicted to the History Channel, what does that say? And how do people watch? Is it TV watching over dinner, or is there a discrete TV watching room?

And then there are computer games. How are they different? Good for the mind? Increase spatial awareness or simply increase competitive aggressiveness?

The jury is still out because TV watching presents genuinely difficult questions. Many factors determine when, where, why and with whom we watch. But most do feel that while television has many advantages, it also can be a social problem. The question, as with so many pleasures, is where to draw the line between healthy and unhealthy consumption patterns.

Unorthodox sales training

Sales people: born or made? This question is often applied to leaders and has been debated for centuries. Interestingly we appear not to consider the same issue for artists, musicians or scientists. We seem to assume a degree of special giftedness that cannot be trained.

So what is it about business? Selectors tend to say people are born *not* made, while trainers clearly think people are born *and* made. Both bring their bias, skills and experience to the question.

Of course, there are more extreme positions within each camp. Thus the "radical selector" is an immutable essentialist who believes that adults can't or won't change and need to have a very specific "talent profile" (probably genetically based) to do the job. They – and they alone – fit the spec and need to be found.

The "radical trainer" on the other hand is an "everything is possible" supporter believing that with the right courses, mentors and coaching practically anybody can be taught to do anything in business. Especially in sales. *Anybody* can be taught to sell *anything*, *anytime*, to *any* customers.

Most of us would support neither extreme. The slightly more pessimistic, who no doubt prefer to call themselves experienced realists, probably err on the selector's end, believing you certainly need some abilities, attitudes or aptitudes to do the job that are not acquirable in training. The moderate training perspective probably argues that with a little effort nearly everybody can be taught how to sell – it's not that difficult and indeed can be a lifestyle.

Whatever your position, few would dispute that all sales people need training. There are selling skills. And there are no shortages of gurus eager to lighten your billfold for the experience of their evangelical mission and message. There are techniques and theories but few can't be comprehensively précised on one sheet of letter size paper.

What courses should you offer? In-house training offers a lot of product knowledge stuff; a bit of non-verbal, body language and neuro-linguistic programming; a few clever questions possibly even scripted; and a video-taped roleplay. A two-case course and you are ready for action. It's all very superficial.

Perhaps salespeople could easily enough pick up the requisite skills from courses or workshops not aimed at salespeople, but teaching the same skills more thoroughly and more sensitively. Consider the following trilogy:

- *Counseling skills* – Nearly everyone believes they are a "good listener." Paradoxically it is often the most interpersonally deaf and nuance-insensitive that have most faith in their skill. Counseling is about being perceptive, about empathy, about understanding. It is essentially about trying to get into the skin of another person to understand how they experience the world. It is about emotional literacy; about timing; and even about courage.

  Let your salespeople attend a short course in counseling devised by a marriage counseling service, a suicide or other hotline. That should sort the wheat from the chaff and teach some really good skills.
- *Acting* – Certainly the car showroom, the beauty counter and the show home are a stage. Selling is theatre. You master your script, you put on your costume, you respond to the audience. Customers need to believe in you as much as your product. You need to keep the faith; live the dream – blah, blah, blah. Acting is about understanding your role. It's about timing and choice of words. It's also about understanding drama.

  Never underestimate sales demonstration drama. It needs careful scripting and good acting.
- *Negotiating skills* – Unlike those in the Grand Bazaar in Istanbul we don't openly haggle. Goods have their price tag and we choose to buy or not. Maybe. That is less and less true for "big objects": cars, houses, jewelry. There are cash discounts, last-day-of-sale offers and so on. Many people have tumbled to this and some have a natural negotiation style.

  Negotiation is about "getting to yes" by use of various strategies of which there are many. Most participants report how much they enjoyed and benefited from their negotiation skills course because they see its wide applicability.

So, sales training now has a bit on product knowledge but consists of three off-site short courses run by people *not* in the business of selling widgets, or anything else. Three or four days of training with counselors, actors and negotiators should do the trick.

USP and RHP

What do you want from a hotel room? Clean and quiet? Reasonable non-ripoff? Internet connections or wifi? Free water and fruit, perhaps? Do you really care if there is a Corby trouser press? But you might like an iron and tea-making facilities. Why are there always mini-bars, but not always tea and coffee facilities? You want the equipment to work and you want it to be user friendly.

And what do you want at your filling station? Do you care about the brand? Unlikely. You simply want the pumps to work and the cashier to be civil and helpful.

A USP is a *unique selling proposition*. An RHP is *a reliable, honest promise*. While customers *want* RHPs, they are all too often *offered* USPs. For marketing guys the sexy words are brand experience, exclusivity, image and innovation, but for most consumers they are affordable, convenient, reliable.

Perhaps it all results from the people who are attracted to marketing. Is it, as the psychologists, say, an issue of selection, or socialization, or both? That is, are fashion-conscious, other-worldly, arty-farty people attracted to marketing, or is it that sensible, sane individuals pick up the strange beliefs and practices of marketing people while working there – or both?

Despite all the money spent on market research, it seems the marketing people may not have heard the simple message of the average customer. In their book called *Simply Better*, Barwise and Meehan (2004) challenge some marketing myths. Their basic point is that marketers don't really understand the desires of their customers.

Start with the simplest question. Parsimoniously, honestly and accurately list the fundamental benefits which your product or service delivers to your key customer. Come on, it's not that difficult! Take their role.

The problem is that marketers really "live the brand." They really care – and they think we do too. They think we are strongly brand-loyal. That we can and do differentiate on the basis of brand; that we always seek new and innovative features on all products. Of course, some people do. They appear naïvely, gullibly, insanely wedded to a brand, though on blind tasting they may not be able to differentiate it.

One reason why the brand guys get it wrong results from their research. Many rely on focus groups which are tasked to answer certain questions. But are they the right questions? Who actually decides?

One central question concerns the issue of innovation and change. We all know from personal experience that habits are difficult to change. We also know that many of us strongly resist change at work and change in our private lives. And the older (and richer) we become the more we are threatened by change.

Master some new complicated technology and the clever, innovative whizz-kids change the system to give us more options, make it more secure or more "user-friendly." Did you want any of them? No. Hence the joy some people take in product consistency and simplicity.

Some of the most obvious things are the most important. Years ago a group that owned a chain of bars did a study to predict what factor or factors were most closely related to profitability. Was it car-parking? The number of "guest beers," or the jukebox? Was it the availability of food, or the charm of the staff? It turned out to be the cleanliness of the toilets. Cleanliness, you see, brought women in, lack of it seriously put them off. It was also an index of management.

You know that certain product managers and marketing guys have lost the plot when you look at their advertising. They seem to think you capture awareness, interest and therefore billfold share by clever-clever, pretty advertising. They worry about adding prestige to the brand and they worry about brand differentiation.

They should spend more time understanding the relatively simple needs of consumers when they make big or small purchases. Yes consumers have lots of choice. Yes, they are influenced by price. Yes, one has to appeal to things like pride and avarice.

But what people want of products is that they be reliable, clean and easy to use. They want advertisers' promises (if they understand them) to be fulfilled. They want RHP not USP.

Reference

Barwise, P. and Meehan, S. (2004) *Simply Better: Winning and Keeping Customers by Delivering What Matters Most*. Boston, MA: Harvard Business School Press.

Work addictions

Thank God it's Monday! People seem pretty divided about their attitude to working hours. A vocal, vociferous, often trade-union-inspired group laments our slavish dedication to work. The long-hours culture destroying health, happiness, family life, and life itself.

The data show that we work many fewer hours than our parents or grandparents. Some have defined excessive working hours as over 48 per week. In the Industrial Revolution a 60-hour week was the norm. Most data from Western countries have shown a steady decrease over the past fifty years, particularly for less-educated blue-collar workers. Interestingly there has been a slight increase for educated, professional, pale males.

But there are those who apparently thrive at work. They volunteer to stay on not on overtime, but for the joy of the activity. No work–life balance for them. Being balanced is staying at work where there is order, support, achievement.

There is evidence (mainly from blue-collar workers) that long hours are bad both for the individual and for the company. Poor physical and mental health, accidents and poor decisions. Some empirical data induced that a 60-hour week increased accidents by a third.

But of course it does depend on the job. The demands–control model is simple to grasp and very important. It differentiates between demands on time, effort, concentration and so on and control over when, how, where, and so on you work. So we have the best (low demands, high control) through passive (low on both) and active (high, high) to the worst (high demands, low control). In these last high-strain jobs, overtime is a demand, a requirement.

Tired employees often find it hard to relax. In order to "come down" quickly they may abuse alcohol and eat badly. They see less of friends and family who may be their best source of social support and who turn quite quickly into a major additional source of stress.

But try telling that to the highly committed, achievement-oriented, dedicated worker. There seem to be four motives for voluntary long hours and hard work:

- Work as its own reward, work as fun, pleasure, intrinsically satisfying.

- Work as emotional respite from home: a calm, undemanding place of emotional stability, predictability and order compared with the very opposite at home.
- Work–leisure tradeoff where you have to work hard to earn the money needed to spend on expensive, but ultimately very satisfying leisure.
- Social contagion, where everyone around works incredibly long hours, making it seem quite normal.

Others have distinguished between the addict and the enthusiast. Addicts feel driven, enthusiasts not. It all depends on drive. Workaholics can be obsessive-compulsive, perfectionistic or achievement-oriented. The first two have problems, the last less so. In essence then, one can be an adjusted, happy, functional workaholic (rather rare) or the sad, dysfunctional, angry, unhappy type.

But when is a heavy worker a workaholic? It's the same definitional problem with booze. At what point, and with what behaviors, is it thought of as seriously and unhealthily addictive? It could be defined in terms of amount. Over fifty hours per week and you're an addict. This would make a terrifying number of us (helpless) addicts. Others provide a more psychological definition:

- Those who devote more time, attention and thought to their work than the situation demands.
- Those who become emotionally crippled and addicted to approval, control, power and success.
- Those with a chronic inability to regulate work habits and overindulge in work to the exclusion of all else.
- Those compelled or driven to overwork by inner pressures, despite low enjoyment at the tasks.

Studies on workaholics showed they held various beliefs: "Work is about win–lose not win–win." "Nice guys finish last." "You prove yourself at work." They strive against others and certain targets.

Needless to say many workaholics have lower psychological wellbeing, poor extra-work relationships and near-disastrous family functioning.

The work enthusiast is different from the work-addict. The latter have lower self-esteem and feel they need to prove themselves. They believe their organization disapproves of a good work–life balance. They feel driven. They work in ways which increase work stress for themselves and others. The workaholic: inadequate, non-delegating, perfectionistic, friendless control freak?

Of course workaholism can be triggered and maintained by job insecurity, limited career opportunities, work overload, understaffing and a competitive corporate culture.

So should we have clinics, drying-out centers for recovering workaholics? Should we sit around in circles supporting each other to do "one day at a time"? Should we swear to be home at 18:00, laptopless and baby-bath-oriented? Should we condemn the workaholic and tax overtime?

Better perhaps to look at the characteristics of the work enthusiast and to discover what it takes to be a happy hard worker for the benefit of all.

End piece – whither managerial psychology?

Of course, there are academics who research all the problems outlined in this book. Though many disciplines are involved, one that is growing rapidly is managerial psychology, populated by applied psychologists of many different backgrounds. They write learned (and popular) books and papers. They propose models and offer solutions. Some are despised by hardbitten managers at the coalface as idle idealists who never get their hands dirty or who have little real-world practical personal experience of things they write about. Other see them as useful, disinterested observers who can help make sense of the complexity of their worlds.

Consultants often claim to be "in touch" with current research. There are lots of popular books which quote academic researchers. And there are "middle-stream" journals between the heavy technical and often near-impenetrable writings of serious academics and magazine articles that attempt to make academic research more accessible. But if you want to know what the researchers are really thinking it is important to look at the academic journals. What in effect do they show?

First, it should be admitted that the term *managerial psychology* certainly seems a lot grander than the term *worker psychology*. It almost sounds a right vs. left, capitalist vs. socialist distinction. But management psychology is not about managers so much as about management. It is probably true however that most managerial psychology is about literate, white-collar workers who can and will complete questionnaires and do interviews, which inevitably may restrict its generalizability. Few studies look at unskilled workers; few studies (still) are done in Third World countries; fewer studies look at what people do (actual behavior) rather than what they (or others) say they do.

Managerial psychology is about how organizations are managed and the consequences for the organization and all its stakeholders. It is about leadership and followership. It is about how people get together to achieve tasks. It is about productivity and satisfaction.

Managerial psychology is a branch of applied psychology as is educational or counseling psychology. Inevitably, then, managerial psychology is something of a hybrid subdiscipline. Its advocates, theoreticians and practitioners are a diverse group of individuals. It is therefore often difficult to get a sense of progress, or indeed lack thereof, in the field. Diversity can lead to tension. There is certainly evidence of disagreement, distrust and disregard between researchers and practitioners who come from different traditions. However, many – not only Hegelians – would see this dialectic process as positive: synthesis arises from thesis and antithesis. That is, the tension from point and counterpoint is the energy that stimulates inquiry and curiosity. Paradigm-challenging is seen as the stuff of advancement. Nothing like a serious "academic spat" to help get to the heart of a problem.

Occasionally anniversaries provoke such reflection. Thus fifty or twenty years after a famous book or paper appeared there may be a "get-together" of researchers in that area to celebrate and critique development and progress. Similarly calendar events like the end or the beginning of a decade, century or millennium offer a good excuse to reflect and ponder.

Management psychologists are magpie-like in the way they steal ideas from other disciplines. They shamelessly "borrow" ideas from evolutionary psychology and from neuroscience and try to show how they are applicable to management. They are often very sensitive to the zeitgeist and able to "package" new (and some old) ideas so that they will be received and well understood by current readers.

Another way the field is reviewed and assessed is the publishing of books on key management thinkers or "gurus" in the area. Or there is the grand historical overview. Others have done similarly but less reverently by looking at buzzwords and fads on a historical basis.

It is easy to offer a critique of both business-school-taught organizational behavior (OB) and traditional, university-based, organizational or work psychology (WP), equally called managerial psychology.

Critiques of OB included:

- *Bandwagoning, faddism and political correctness* – Jumping onto fashionable concepts, processes, theories, irrespective of the academic proof and rigor while ignoring issues and evidence that appear less palatable to clients.
- *Preferring case-studies and anecdotes to data* – Relying on case-studies to illustrate issues rather than providing robust, empirical and behavioral evidence in support.
- *Having few powerful, explanatory theories* – Being more reliant on buzzwords, doctrinaire statements and poorly documented case-studies

than investing in the development and testing of theories of how and why people behave as they do in organizations.

- *Having exclusively derivative methodology* – Not appearing to be interested in measurement or analysis of obviously complex and dynamic systems.
- *Having an unclear identity* – In the most fundamental sense not being either a discipline or a subdiscipline by not being able to forge an identity that has boundaries.
- *Stressing marketing over-development* – Being very good at marketing courses, books and conferences without spending as much effort actually developing a research agenda.
- *Focusing on popular, rather than important, issues* – Giving a sense of achievement and progress by choosing tradable, simple modern problems, not the important and inevitably difficult ones.

But what of the themes in modern management psychology? If one studies the journals in the area it is possible to pinpoint various issues.

The individual vs. the group tension

At the heart of many managerial questions are differences in perspectives between three different approaches. Differential and personality theorists seek to explain behavior such as team or organizational success (morale, productivity) and failure (absenteeism, accidents) in terms of personality traits, temperaments and dispositions. They are essentially individual-difference theorists. Individuals' makeup and temperament are at the heart of business success and failure.

On the other hand, social psychologists stress the power of situational forces like corporate climate and culture and their role in shaping people inside organizations. They are always particularly interested in strong situations, which appear to coerce maladaptive behavior such as counterproductive behaviors in the workplace. There are not good and bad people but structures and processes that lead people to behave in these particular ways.

Third, sociologists stress societal factors. They point out that organizations are embedded in the wider society whose forces are such as to shape individuals, groups and whole organizations. Thus they compare First and Third Worlds, East vs. West, developing vs. developed societies, noting their impact on organizational development.

Of course all three are correct. The trick is seeing how they are related to one another. Thus appraising how a bright, narcissistic manager might behave in a struggling multinational in South Africa surely necessitates a full understanding of the person, the organization and the culture.

Work-specific vs. out-of-work behavior

If the day can be divided, it is possible to argue that we spend around a third at work, a third asleep and a third doing something else. What you do outside work inevitably effects how to behave in the workplace. Known as the *work–life balance* issue, it is an area of research but little real debate.

Many organizations ask, explicitly or implicitly, for total allegiance, engagement and commitment from their staff. They ask them always to "go the extra mile" and they exhort the virtue of loyalty. They like to believe that a person's life should and does revolve entirely around their work. Work not only brings monetary rewards but a total package of psychological benefits from a profound sense of identity to a source of creativity and mastery. You live to work, not work to live. Work is a crusade: it must be an all-encompassing passion. It is very much the mantra of a macho, 1980s perspective.

This has procured a significant backlash from those who resent any organization having the effrontery to believe they own both your soul and your free time. Using the loaded and probably inaccurate term "life" as opposed to "work," the "work–life balance" supporters argue not only that organizations have no right to "eat into" or "colonize" your non-work time but also that a healthy balance leads to a healthier individual. It has become a feminine issue and has been championed by many such that it is now "politically correct" to support the idea.

But it must be true that private commitments to family and friends, that personal recreations (both healthy and unhealthy) and that preferred "leisure time" activities must all impact on how people work – from their absenteeism to the accident rate and from their professionalism to their productivity.

The science vs. practitioner tension

In all the areas of applied psychology like clinical or educational psychology there is always a tension between the academic scientists and the consultant practitioners. Frequently the tension is so great that there are two societies or divisions representing their different interests. Consultants complain that academic research addresses trivial, irrelevant or too complex problems. Further, their criteria of importance are certainly not those of clients. Academics on the other hand are swift to point out all the (many) limitations in the "research" of consultants, which include such things as very small or biased samples, no control groups, excessive use of self-report questionnaires, use of out-of-date measures and complete lack of statistical sophistication.

Occasionally researchers attempt a "marriage" between those driven to derive models or processes and those who want some practical advice regarding what to do with all the complications and implications of model development. The research scientists say they seek to understand first and then (possibly) make recommendations afterwards. The practitioners want to act now albeit with imprecise or partial knowledge. Inevitably some are more tolerant of ambiguity than others. The two worlds attract very different types with different aims and ambitions and skills and preferences. No wonder, then, they are often so distrustful of one another.

The bright-side (healthy, optimistic) vs. dark-side (unhealthy, pessimistic) tension

It is said that until the "birth" of positive psychology, psychologists wrote one hundred books on depression for every one on happiness. They seemed not very interested in the causes of happiness but much more on its opposite. They appeared to believe happiness was not always an issue, a state or a condition worth investigating. They did not see it as a problem. It was like health or wellness. You always put your effort into studying the illness, unhappiness, failure.

To some extent the opposite is, or was, the case in management psychology. Certainly if one considers popular management books they seem to present a relentlessly simple, positive view on the "business of management." The process of management is portrayed as straightforward and managers as swashbuckling heroes. They tend to emphasize the positive nature of people, the relative ease of change and universality of the management process. Many are even evangelical in their tone and content.

However there is now a serious interest in what may be called the dark side of behavior at work (Furnham and Taylor 2004). This is concerned with when, why and how management derailment occurs. It examines in detail individual pathology which leads to organizational failure. The literature tends to be dominated by a clinical and individual-differences perspective.

Dark-side issues are explored in different ways. There is a growing and fascinating literature on personality disorders in managers and how they lead to derailment. There is also a longstanding interest in all the negative features at work, like the causes of absenteeism, accidents, stress and turnover. For the first time there is an emergence of leadership books on those who "cock up" rather than conquer; who cause the share price to plummet rather than increase; who end up sacked or imprisoned rather than lionized. For the first time people are becoming aware of the necessity to look for *select-out* processes rather than exclusively *select-in* ones. The Peter Pan world is now a little wise and skeptical about the whole business of management.

The quality vs. quantity, modernist vs. postmodernist tension

Management psychologists are diverse in their interests, training and approaches. They are also usually fairly pragmatic and eclectic in the methodologies they use. While few are particularly sophisticated, the last twenty years have seen some powerful epistemological rifts between different camps.

This is manifest partly in the quant-vs.-qual divide which may represent a richer, more profound divide between empiricism and relativism. That is, epistemology informs methodology.

Management research has also experienced the postmodernist, anti-empirical critique. It is the anti-Enlightenment attack on truth. The postmodernists are by and large against research at all.

The quant–qual issue is often about the purpose of the research. Quantitative people speak to the richness of their data; to the way it reveals complex and subtle and counterintuitive ideas and processes. Qualitative people talk about representative samples, about modeling real-world data and testing hypotheses. The advent of structural equation modeling as well as access to longitudinal data banks has completely transformed the quality of qualitative research because it has allowed a real exploration of multivariate causal patterns.

The two sides can be seriously bitchy about each other. But most know that the methodology follows from the questions asked. The quant-jocks see the qual-babes as doing a spot of pilot research; while the latter see great models constructed on simple-minded survey research. There is a healthy *via media* between the two.

Fairness vs. efficiency tensions

For many years there has been a passionate debate between advocates of equity in the workplace. This is often about identifying all the stakeholders in the workplace and trying to ensure an optimal balance between their different needs.

The *caveat emptor*, profit-maximizing school sees the duty of managers to maximize returns for shareholders, customers and employees while staying within the law. For them morality and ethics are not business issues. Managers should concentrate in open and free competition, without fraud or deception, to produce goods and services as efficiently and effectively as possible.

On the other hand there are more and more advocates and researchers in business ethics who believe in other principles like the charity principle, the stewardship principle, the idea of *noblesse oblige*. They are cognizant of the large number of stakeholders in all businesses, of the wide "duties" of any company to the society in which it is located and also of issues around fairness in the workplace. Stress is on equality over equity; of fairness over efficiency; of health and happiness over productivity.

On one side are the work–life balance, diversity, personal-growth advocates who seem most concerned with job satisfaction, equality and fairness while on the other are the cold-gray men of the bottom line who note that profitability in an ever increasingly competitive environment is the only way to survive let alone prosper.

The universal vs. the culture-specific tension

For some the management of individuals, like parenting, is pretty well fundamental and universal. That is there are some rudimentary but important pointers to how to manage. Set people clear but attainable targets; support them in achieving them, give them regular feedback and reward success.

Universalists assert that management processes are essentially the same in Addis Ababa, Antwerp and Atlanta. They celebrate cross-cultural replication but essentially hold that theories, processes and explanations are invariant across time and place. They assert the 'twas-ever-thus school of thinking and may therefore rejoice in the unity of mankind.

Anthropologists and cross-cultural psychologists on the other hand have as their *raison d'être* the concept of difference variability. They are eager to point out how national, religious and corporate culture makes all the difference. Their retort is more likely to be "Yes, but not among the Bonga Bonga" – meaning that things "work differently" in different cultures. Some enjoy cross-cultural comparisons while others believe that is essentially impossible because of the number and complexity of mediating and moderating variables.

Other tensions

Within psychology and the other social sciences in general, there are of course many other tensions, some going back many years. Thus one could list the following:

- *Affect vs. cognition* – That is, heart vs. head, sometimes (erroneously) portrayed as left- and right-brained thinking. Management science has been dominated from the cognitive perspective with extensive investigations into judgement, decision-making and so on and neglecting the important role of emotions at work. This may be in part responsible for the great interest in emotional vs. academic tension.
- *Case-studies vs. representational research* – A great interest in neuroscience has made the study of individuals quite acceptable. Whereas in the business world of management psychology the case-study approach usually consisted of hagiographic biographies of high-profile business men or historical inquiries into great thinkers. Most researchers demand nomothetic as opposed to idiographic research with its possibilities of extrapolation to larger populations. However, there does seem to be a growth in the acceptability of case-studies.
- *Social science vs. neuroscience* – The relatively sudden but profound growth in neuroscience with its powerful methodologies is beginning to have its effects felt in management psychology. Some from a more traditional and oldfashioned social-science background have rejected what has been called "electrophrenology," while others have seen exciting possibilities for development in this area.

Conclusions

First, management psychology is a healthy, growing, vibrant enterprise. There is reason to be joyful and optimistic. Managerial psychology has kept abreast of developments in theory and methodology. More than that, it is not simply derivative from, and therefore dependent on, other disciplines for its theory methodology. It has a definable mission and identity. There is a real sense of progress.

Second, it is a diverse operation from three perspectives, where diversity is healthy and adaptive. It is certainly an international enterprise. Researchers from all over the world share common problems and methods to investigate them. It seems that because of the importance and ubiquity of management, people from all over the world are interested in the topic. It is also diverse in the range of topics researched. Many fields are much narrower and more exclusionary than managerial psychology, which by definition of its *raison d'être* has to be inclusive.

Third, management psychology (really) does make a difference. It is easy for academics to remain in their isolated fairy castles poring over complex theories and data sets that seem of little practical use to those in the business of actual management. Management psychology is really an applied science where practical issues drive research agendas and where practitioners look to academic experts for a steer on their politics.

Certainly it is true that these tensions are not evidence of grand theories competing. There are no great tectonic plates overriding one another with earthquake-like, shattering results. But there are those who take different disciplinary and methodological positions that have consequences for how problems are framed and how questions are answered.

What needs to be done next? Management psychology has many stakeholders. But for researchers there seem to be at least three issues that need to be considered. There are dramatic and very important developments in the brain sciences. Over the past decade cognitive neuroscience and behavioral genetics have made impressive progress in many areas. Through ever more sophisticated technology powerful insights are being made regarding how people process information about their world. We are also learning to understand the complex interactions between genes and their environment.

These findings will impact on all the social sciences. Although some, like sociologists and economists, who prefer to understand phenomena at a group level and prefer to aggregate data, may ignore or downplay this work, it is clear that it will have an answer to many problems, ranging from whether, how and when people differentiate brands to whether job satisfaction has a genetic basis. Managerial psychology, a hybrid discipline at best, cannot afford to ignore developments in the brain and neurosciences. At this point in time it looks as if there will be major breakthroughs in our understanding of many issues for all behavioral and social scientists.

But what about the academic response to practical problems? Every organization in the West has a more diversified workforce. Societies are aging and people are working for many more years. Technology has changed, legislation changes how, when and why people do or do not work. Changes in how people work throw up new problems and issues for researchers to investigate. Change in the structure of society has had a great impact on the workplace. New workplace problems and issues call for solutions. Consultants and researchers are asked to help understand then solve problems which often start whole research agendas. For instance, the work–life balance area was a result of more married women working.

Managerial psychology is driven by a pure and an applied agenda. It is therefore not always easy to predict how practical problems will generate research interest. One issue that appears to be gaining considerable attention is that of climate warming and how it can be most effectively dealt with. All sorts of workers are becoming aware of their carbon footprint. They are being induced to change all sorts of behaviors to reduce it. As yet there is no defined academic managerial psychology literature on this topic. However, it is an example of where real-world, practical issues influence research.

The future for managerial psychology looks bright – but that is not an excuse to be complacent.

References

Covey, S. (2004) *The Seven Habits of Highly Effective People*. New York: Free Press.

Crainer, N. (2000) *The Management Century: A Critical Review of the 20th Century Thought and Practice*. San Francisco, CA: Jossey Bass.

Furnham, A. (2004) "The Future (and Past) of Work Psychology and Organisational Behaviour: A Personal View," *Management Revue*, *15*, 420–6.

Furnham, A. and Petrides, K. (2006) Deciding on Promotions and Redundancies. *Journal of Managerial Psychology*, *21*, 6–18.

Furnham, A. and Taylor, J. (2004) *The Dark Side of Behaviour at Work*. Basingstoke: Palgrave.

Kennedy, C. (1991) *Guide to the Management Gurus*. London: Century.